The Communication Course

Frederick Dodson

Copyright © 2014 Frederick Dodson

All rights reserved

CONTENTS

1 Introduction
2 Energy Exchange
3 Authenticity and Integrity
4 How to Stop Fear
5 Communication Excellence
6 Public Speaking
7 Presence

1
Introduction

This is a Course Manual for the improvement of your communication, charisma, assertiveness, presence, authenticity, integrity, word-power, speech, vocabulary and voice.
Life is not about the physical world, it is about the people inhabiting it and the energy they exchange. You can accumulate gold, hug trees and surf waves, but if you're alone all the time, none of it is fun. Your state improves in proportion to how many meaningful connections you have to others. The state of the world improves when we become better communicators.

This Manual is not suitable for conventional academic or corporate settings because it openly uses spiritual terms that are rooted in consciousness research. Communication that is only understood as a matter of speech or images is severely limited. This misconception comes from the currently dominant, sophomoric worldview that a human being "is a brain and a body" rather than consciousness equipped with soul and an energy-field. Half of all communication is invisible! It is the energy exchanged between people. So-called "Communication Courses" that censor anything to do with spirituality or energy-fields are missing half the story.
To benefit from this book you should use a marker to highlight parts that are relevant to you. Then, once you have finished, re-read the highlighted parts and

find a way to put them into practice. The map is not the territory. But that which you train yourself to do has a lasting effect on your personality.

2
Energy Exchange

Energy Fields

You may not be able to tell your life story in 10 seconds, but people can sense it because it's all stored in your aura. You walk around with an energy-field, a wide circumference around your physical body, invisible to the eye but immediately sensed by all. Everything you have ever done, thought and experienced in your life is stored there. Who you are cannot be masked by words, make-up and how you dress. Those things will improve your overall aura but they can't cover-up your Essence. In other words you can easily tell whether someone has led a life of crime on the streets or grew up cozy and pampered. They could both be wearing the same suit, but they would have a different "feel". Beyond the age of 40 you also start seeing a persons' lifestyle in their faces.

Your mere presence changes the mood of any given place. You could be in a room, remain silent and you`d still influence the people there. Your personal presence is either of benefit or not. Your negativity is best let go of the instant it arises, because you cannot really hide it. For example, if you have an argument with someone and think "But I did't say anything bad to him!" you may have nonetheless radiated something bad. For the eyes and ears there are many secrets, but to your sixth sense nothing is a secret.

So how can you make that personal energy field brighter and stronger? Through kindness. Radiating hostility attracts some real dangers into your field, as well as ill health and bad finances, whereas kindness attracts some real blessings. Goodwill is the basis of effective Communication. Problems should be tackled immediately before they build a nest in your aura. As long as you try to escape them they will keep coming back in a new guise, so solve everything in consciousness first and instantly. Also, cutting your connections to any associations, organizations and people that foster too much negativity will brighten your light.

Elevating your own level of consciousness counterbalances the negativity of thousands. Then your presence in an airplane and intentions for a safe-flight influence the trip of everyone on that plane. That's how you are directly responsible for the wellbeing of everyone there, you are indeed "your brother's keeper". See how that feels the next time you are sitting around at an airport in the mistaken assumption that nobody else has anything to do with you.

A disturbed or depressed auric field emanates a cold energy. That is a cold that can be physically felt and measured on a Thermometer. You could actually stretch out your hand and feel the pockets of cold. When such an energy-field is walking near you, you get a chill. What those people require is professional help and a whole lot of warmth...in the form of loving kindness. The lower states of consciousness are actually not hellfire and brimstone, but rather ice. Ice would make a better symbol of hell than fire. This hell-on-earth is a frozenness of feeling, a self-absorption, a contraction, a hardness of heart. And that is why it is good for you to walk around with an energy field shining warmly, openly, glowingly...because just being in that state helps countless of people without you even having to talk to them, deal with them or even spend time. Just walking past someone who is suffering and providing a smile or non-verbal well-wishes can dissolve their stuck-ness right then and there. You can be an angel to others. Once you have gone beyond seeking love and approval and start giving it is when your start to shine.

With a strong and bright aura is that you no longer have to protect yourself from negativity. Protection is only required at mid-levels of energy, not at the higher ones. Where there is no fear (coldness) but only love (warmth) there is no more danger because no real harm can happen. As you realize you are an energy-field and not a body, you start feeling invincible...not physically invincible, but invincible as that which you really are.

Those familiar with a knowledge more arcane know that the warmth of your energy field can become so intense that it too can be physically felt and measured. That warmth is different than the normal warmth given off by the body. It's a warmth that can heal colds, as you will have noticed when you take care of loved ones who have colds.

Being is even more important than Doing. When you are visiting with people or standing in a cue or when you are sitting at home or driving a car you can realize that what you are being is more important than what you are doing. Instead of asking yourself "Am I saying the right thing?", first check what you are Being. Instead of asking yourself "What are we going to do?" adjust who-you-are-going-to-be. If you are someone who frequents a subway, train-station or airport when you go to work, you have plenty of opportunity to experiment with these ideas. People will respond more to you're Being than Doing. You will radiate a different Being-ness on different days, even if your doing-ness of purchasing a ticket, getting on the plane, etc. remains the same.

Here's a secret that will change your life: Rather than being concerned with how people see you, be concerned for their well-being. That will shift your aura radically and your presence will fill the whole plane, train, room.

Exercise: Take a walk in your neighborhood, in town or in your offices and deliberately radiate kindness and fascination. Externalize your awareness fully. Continue to do so for at least 30 minutes or more. Take note of how you feel afterwards and how others responded to your presence.

Emotional Contagion

Joy is contagious. But of course it's not only joy - all emotions and states are transferred among people. Your anger is felt by others, even if you try to hide it. If your walk through town you might pick up on the crowds overall vibration and feel kind of sleepy when you get home. You can feel whether your spouse is in a good mood or not, before you even enter the room.

You could even feel this if you weren't present. Most communication really is non-verbal, sensed before even saying a word. Even sexual arousal is contagious, so you best be careful where and when you feel it (hence, looking after your own sexual arousal instead of that of your partner will make for better sex for both involved). Knowing for certain that your state is transferred to everyone around you and anyone you are holding in mind, has you feel more responsible. Your emotions are not as private as you think they are.

Psychologists are well aware of this and call it "Emotional Contagion" and have proven the existence of such in countless double-blind studies. Unfortunately, because modern Academia suppresses everything even remotely spiritual, they are not permitted to say why and how this happens - by vibration, by energy! So they`ll say that "because of the chemical reactions of the emotions, a person emits a certain smell and this smell is picked up by other people". Or they`ll say "subtle body-language cues are communicated and picked up by others and that's how emotions are transferred". I obviously disagree. While emotions do influence body-language and body-odor, those are not the only things that are going on. For the last 20 years it has been my profession to shift peoples moods and if necessary without words, body-language or smell. I have witnessed entire rooms full of people emotionally shifted because of a person's presence. I have seen them shifted both up and down. When I am in a bad mood, my seminars are lacking, even if I do the best to hide it. If I am in a good mood, my seminars skyrocket, no matter what I say or do.

When I was in my early twenties I would take the subway and experiment with "breathing in" and then holding different emotional states and then see how the surrounding people react. One of my favorite exercises in this regard, was to pump myself up with the energy of Humor. I would intend "Humor" and fill up my body, imagining that I am breathing all the Humor of the Universe in (imagining nothing on the out-breathe to keep the energy in-body). I`d go on for minutes. Funny thoughts would come to mind, but the experiment involved not laughing, not smiling, not showing anyone any sign of how I felt. I would sit there almost bursting with hilarity while keeping a straight face. This strong emanation always had a remarkable effect on the people sitting around me. Some of them would begin smiling or snicker for no apparent reason, their faces would lighten up, many of them would look over to me because they could sense "something" happening.

Because of a widespread awareness of emotional contagion (despite it not being taught in school), people often ask how they can protect themselves from negative vibes. My response is, that the best protection is to increase your own emotional state, to release you own anxieties and resentments. Sure, you can picture a protective aura around yourself, but that method is weaker than simply improving yourself. Positive states are stronger than negative ones and will neutralize anything mucky coming at you. Sure, if you are bombarded with negativity 24/7, that should be able to get you back down. But a bit higher on the emotional scale, nothing can bog you down, distract you or get you tired. Nothing at all. So a good mix of releasing your own inner darkness and not spending too much time in harsh environments are more than enough protection. One day you reach a state where no protection is required and then the purpose of your presence is to sooth those around you.

Exercise: Try to covertly radiate positive emotions at someone. Don't strain yourself in doing so, just let a sense of appreciation or humor flow in their direction. You`ll first have to generate this feeling within yourself. You can do so my thinking or remembering things you love or find funny. Then, simply imagine non-verbally transferring those emotions to another person. Notice whether and how they respond. Continue to practice this until you get a sense of what influence your mere emotional state has.

Energy Exchange

People are walking, talking spheres of energy, not just physical pieces of meat. As such, we exchange energy on a daily basis. Here is an incomplete list of how we exchange energy with others, from low to high intensity.

* Being physically close
* Conversation
* Eye Contact
* Handshake
* Hugging
* Kissing
* Sex

Here is a list of different types of greetings and the energy-exchange from low to high intensity:

* Namaste Greeting
* Bowing
* High Five
* Handshake
* Hugging
* Kissing

If two people of good energy meet, then energy-exchange is desirable. But it's not always desirable because we are not always in good energy. Some think that "hugging people" is universally a positive thing. But if someone's inner turmoil is severe, you don't necessarily want to hug them; unless your own level is so good that you are immune to their negativity. Or unless you wish to take on their energy to help them. So you're at a funeral and you allow someone who is grieving to hug you. Your care will help them release some of their grief. I have found that if you love the grieving person you are hugging, there will be no loss of energy. Love really does make you immune. If however you do not like a person and you take on their grief by hugging them, there will be an energy-transfer leaving you more tired afterwards. It is not the grief-energy itself but you're resistance toward the person that's expending energy. If you live your life by the motto "Love All, Serve All", you can handshake and hug anyone without energy loss and every connection you make will be an energy-gain for both sides.

In a recent seminar I shook the hands of more than a 100 students. But it was no problem for me because both I and the students were of generally "good energy". If I had to do the same thing in downtown to a bunch of strangers it would have probably left me slightly tired and in need of a shower. In India they greet you without touch, using the "Namaste" sign. In Japan they use "Bowing". These are "safe" greetings that don't involve much exchange. The advantage is that no negative energy is transferred. The disadvantage is that intentions are concealed. Touch transmits your energy and thereby some of your and the others intentions (people who want to hide their intentions never touch). So we use handshakes to indicate trustworthiness and connection. The handshake itself can establish a connection that was not there before.

Unless you are in good energy (and thereby mostly immune to negativity), you`ll want to be choosy about the people who associate with on a regular basis or have sex with. Sex is one of the ultimate ways of mixing energies. Of course the energy-influence from others only makes up a fraction of our personal overall energy-state (perhaps 15%) and does not trump the influence of your own thoughts and emotions, nutrition, sports and lifestyle. So while it's good to be aware of your exchange with others, there is no reason to exaggerate its meaning to a point where you start blaming others for negative energy. If you are energy-less others may have something to do with that, but your own thoughts have more to do with it.

Should it happen that you pick up "negative vibes" from others, washing your hands or taking a shower is a good way to cleanse yourself. Taking showers not only cleans the physical skin but also accumulated vibrations (even more than taking a bath, which tends to let the washed off energy linger in the tub). This is why, after mediocre love-making we feel the urge to take a shower and after good love-making we do not want to shower for a while. This is why, when we are feeling really good, we prefer not to shower, in order to keep the energy and when we are exhausted, a shower feels so refreshing.

As long as we live on earth are surrounded by positive, neutral, negative energy. Of course we are even influenced by people without touching them. We all have been in the presence of people where the room feels so dense that we just want to get out fast as possible. And we have also been in the presence of people where we wanted to stay as long as possible. The most common approaches to negative energy have been fight or flight. These seem to be genetically hardwired into our nervous system. Our "normal" reaction is either to put up force, to fight it (thereby descending to its level) or escape and remove ourselves (thereby not solving but only postponing it). When we do not know whether to fight or flight, we freeze up. A frozen state produces many different problems including the inability to articulate, the inability to relax, the inability to make love and difficulty to concentrate.

When really grave threats are present "fight or flight" makes sense. But most events we encounter in daily life are not that dangerous. Fight or Flight is often unnecessary and yet we respond to many harmless events as if things were a matter of life and death. It is not helpful to respond to negativity or perceived negativity as if you were warding off lethal snakes in the jungle.

Anyone interested in psycho-spiritual maturation will practice reducing fight-or-flight responses and develop other ways of dealing with negativity. So I repeat: The best way to immunize yourself against threats, attacks and negativity is to ascend your own mood level. Radiating love, for example, will melt other people's hardness and cruelty and not allow you to be subject to mistreatment. If you consciously decide that you are not subject to certain surrounding negative influence, you won't be. So it's not the best idea to remove yourself every time the going gets tough. It is a good idea to remove yourself if you are feeling tired, sick or distracted. But if you are well and fit, negative influence is a great opportunity to practice inner calm.

You can run, hide, fight, try to protect yourself, build a wall around yourself, try to make deals and bribes, but in the end the negative influence won't go away unless you increase your own level to a point where you no longer attract such influence into your life. Any act of kindness and forgiveness makes you instantly immune to bad energy. Your self-identification can also make you immune. This is why statistically, police officers are rarely victims of theft, doctors rarely get sick (even though they are surrounded by sick people), bicycle-riders rarely suffer overweight, etc.

The key lies in reducing your first-impulse-reaction. Think back to a time when someone harshly criticized you. Notice how your first impulse may have been to either attack the person back (fight) or go away (flight). Both options are blind to the opportunity offered. Some criticism is valid, some isn't. So the best thing would be to notice your automatic inner reaction, but not to act on it. To stay seated with the person instead of going away and to stay calm instead of attacking back. You would first of all acknowledge the critic and take some time to breathe. Then you may or may not respond, but if you do respond it comes out much stronger and not all frozen up. What happens? You come out of the conversation feeling better instead of energy-depleted. All of life is a game of energy and if you want, you have full control of your reactions and choices.

Exercise: When criticized or confronted, let go of "fight or flight". Instead, do your best to remain poised. Delay your response to whoever is confronting you. If the criticism appears to be invalid, no response at all is needed. If it appears to be valid criticism, fully acknowledge it. Practice this until you get it right and no turbulence is created.

Spiritual Osmosis

"Spiritual Osmosis" is what I call the non-verbal learning that takes place in the presence of a teacher or as the member of a group. It could be anything - a math class, a sports coach, a motorcycle club, a fraternity, a spiritual guru, a dancing class. By being in their presence a transfer of energy takes place that goes beyond the written and spoken lessons of that group or teaching. Who a teacher is, what a teacher lives, what a teacher demonstrates, what a teacher feels partially transfers on to you. That's why you learn much more rapidly in an actual workshop or seminar setting than on the Internet, from a book or from a recording. If you are a member of some group you begin assimilating the mentality, attitude and behavior of that group subconsciously...even if you don't pay attention to what is being said.
The non-verbal transfer of energy is poorly understood by society because it is not yet fully acknowledged that the main thing that goes on between humans is the flow of invisible energy. Whether you join or leave a group depends on how comfortable you feel with a particular group. Good teachers know that it is not enough to convey certain lessons; they also have to represent a certain state of mind and body while teaching. If my own vibratory frequency is no good, it doesn't't matter how smart my words are. If on the other hand I am radiant, I can make plenty of mistakes and people will still learn a whole lot.

Eye-Contact

Every time people meet, energy is exchanged. A little is exchanged when they meet online, much is exchanged when they meet physically and even more when there is eye contact, which is really soul-to-soul contact.

It's silly that this kind of stuff is never taught in school just because "science" doesn't accept the existence of life-force / energy / aura / consciousness. Everyone instinctively knows that eye-contact exchanges the most energy (along with touch), that you feel the most when you look someone in the eye. We also know why city-people tend to avoid eye contact: It's too overwhelming in crowded places. Country-folk tend to be more into eye-contact because not that many people are around. Avoiding eye-contact then, has only two reasons:

* You don't want to be felt
* You don't want to feel others

If you want to avoid detection or if you want to avoid another's energy and emotional state, you avoid eye-contact. In some cases it also has to do with a kind of cultural politeness, with not imposing one's own state on others.

Rather than seeing eye-contact or lack thereof as "good or bad", they simply serve different purposes. Let's say I am at a gathering or party and I want to go "stealth" - not to get into any conversations, not mingle. In that case I would put my head and eyes slightly down so that no eye-contact is made and nobody can read my mood. Eye-contact is the beginning of connection and communication. So those who are shy and those not in the mood for socializing, avoid it. Because your life-energy shines through the eyes, lifting your head, looking around, connecting to other eyes is great non-verbal communication. If you know how to play with your eyes, you don't even have to say anything and will still be viewed as a "good communicator" and "interesting person"...even if you only said a couple of words all evening. It's worthwhile to practice a little bit of eye-communication, to let your eyes become livelier when the occasion calls for it. There are hundreds of things you can "say" just with your eyes. Without uttering a single word your eyes can say:

Yes
No
That's great!
That's strange
Inquisitive
Fun
Boredom
Excitement
Interest
Calm
Compassion
Cunning
Arrogance
Amazement

While I listed those words, could you imagine the

accompanying eyes? When people remember you, they don't only remember what you said, they remember the look in your face. A person with expressive eyes is perceived as being more lively and trustworthy.

When in a lousy mood, sick, angry, fearful or having bad intentions, you'll avoid direct eye-contact because it is through such contact that energy is transferred. When the police interrogate criminals, the criminal will try to mask his lies by deliberately holding eye-contact, because it's an indicator of honesty. However, this will often turn into a glare or stare, thus unmasking the lies. The reason it freezes into a stare is because the liar is trying to keep eye-contact purposefully while holding the energy (not letting it transfer to the interrogator). The husband who has been unfaithful to his spouse, comes home and is quizzed on his whereabouts by his wife can easily be detected by either avoiding eye-contact or by holding frozen eye contact. Super-professional liars would know how to fake natural looking eye movements (in that case only intuition could unmask them).

For "feeling energy", having frequent eye-contact (not as a stare) is preferable. Why? You feel more of life. If you avoid eye-contact all the time you isolate yourself from the flow and exchange of energy that life is. With eye-contact you establish trust, rapport, friendship, humor, joy...the whole array of positive emotions.

So if eye-contact is so positive, then why do some cultures avoid it and consider it impolite? If you have ever read a book on "Intercultural Behavior" you will have learned that each culture has different amounts of "closeness" (=energy exchange) that are deemed appropriate. Russians seem to like to hug and kiss complete strangers while the Japanese won't touch and look. If you look carefully at how Europeans greet vs. how Americans greet you will see that Europeans often, subconsciously, tend to move toward the other or slightly bow their heads or nod, whereas Americans will often stand straight, not moving in the others direction while shaking hands. This subtle difference makes Europeans appear slightly more polite. On the other hand, Americans will smile more often than Europeans which makes Europeans appear slightly cold.

Obviously there are some advantages to keeping ones energy private and not mingling with anyone. The most obvious reason is: Not everybody's energy is so pleasant. Another reason is that privacy is precious. Privacy is so important in our times because the world is full of invasive peering, leering, peeping entities, especially online. Another instance in which eye-contact is not helpful is when you have to think (such as solving some kind of math problem or writing a list of errands). Externalized attention elevates one from the thinking-mode of consciousness, so eye-contact makes internal thinking more difficult. Two lovers staring at each other have disconnected from all rational thought.
But as the consciousness-level of planet earth rises, it will become increasingly safe and pleasant to connect because people's energies will become more healthy and joyous. In some Mediterranean and Mideast

cultures there is the concept of the "evil eye". This concept arose precisely because a lot of energy is transferred through the eyes. So as less and less people look at others with spite, envy, hate or fear, eye-contact will become more common.
Of course eye-contact between a teacher and student surpasses "online courses". If you are, for example, thinking about learning a language online...don't. It goes so much faster in the presence of a real teacher because of all the "subtle energies" transferred through the eyes.

Prolonged eye-contact or holding ones gaze is usually applied in either flirt and romance situations or in spiritual-exercise contexts and acting-schools. Those are the places some intense energy is exchanged. (One other context might be poker games and casinos, where extended eye contact is made to ascertain whether someone is bluffing or not). Whether gaze-holding is sexual or spiritual depends on which chakra ones intentions are coming from. In a flirt situation, the eye-contacts will become longer and longer (and if you at this point are still asking "Are they interested?" you're a fool. Of course they are interested, otherwise eye-contact wouldn't be that long!). In a spiritual context you can actually send healing to the other via the eyes and via holding someone in your attention-field for a long time (giving a person space). You can also transfer various telepathic information as well as view the various identities (past, present and future) of a person.

In extreme situations, understanding eye-energy could be a matter of survival. If you were a prisoner of war,

you would initially avoid eye-contact with your captors and then slowly, over time, increase eye-contact frequency. I won't tell you why, that's something you can figure out yourself.
If your relationship is going south, you can improve it by increasing eye contact. Again, it doesn't take a detective to figure out why.

Most peoples direction-of-attention is linked to where there eyes go. Even though attention is independent of the eyes, most people think they are linked. So if their eyes wander to a certain person, their attention is also there. There is so much power in the eyes that people use it for all sorts of manipulative things...to make people nervous by looking at their bodies instead of faces, to retract eye contact to signal disagreement, to seduce someone through frequent on-and-off gazing, etc. I say "etc." because I don't want to go into all the manipulative ways eyes can be used.

Bottom line: While it's often more comfortable to avoid eye-contact, especially when you don't want to meet strangers, it will contribute to your energy-state if you more often look and connect. And look some more. And maybe just a bit longer. Reality is mostly about the energy-exchange going on between its energy-units (humans). The more you participate in that exchange the more abundant you get.
Here's a nice trick if you want to improve your perception of someone: Imagine them better than you are perceiving them and then transfer that positive mental image onto them. It will be transferred through your eyes and you will experience them in an

improved version. What, they didn't teach you that at school?

Exercise: Increase the general amount of eye-contact you have with people. Notice the improvement of Communication that goes along with it.

3
Authenticity and Integrity

Authenticity

Being Authentic allows you to walk through life without being shy, self-conscious, fearful, grovelling, evasive or unkind. When you are your true self there is an air of confidence, poise and ease about you. Instead of thinking "How do people see me?" and "What do they think of me?" you will be thinking "I am sexy and I know it". Compare those two inner conversations. Compare "I am sexy and I know it" with the usual stream of thoughts you have in daily life.

So how to feel at ease with others most of the time? Well, there are many things I could say about the how-to of this, but you may not remember any of them when you really need them. Being Authentic is not a "Technique" it is the absence of any Technique. Therefore I will summarize how to attain and maintain the state while communicating with others into one sentence:

Crave nothing, resist nothing, state your true intentions without equivocation and externalize your attention and allow yourself to flow a state of gentle Humor.

That's it. That's the whole formula. For some, it can take decades to learn, but sometimes it can also just be there in an instant, just by remembering this statement. The very instant you crave something from another person, you are no longer entirely free, calm and clear. But if I need nothing from them and do not need them to say or do anything in particular, that means you take and accept them exactly as they are right now. That not only allows you to feel at ease, but helps them feel comfortable too and I can tell them the truth of anything. If I don't depend on them to like me, give me money, give me love or anything else, then I am not the least bit shy or awkward or withholding information or seeking approval. On the other side, I resist nothing either. If they are awkward or uncomfortable that does not bother me, I do not resist it. I either go somewhere else or send them waves of appreciation to help improve their state. Too much preoccupation with how others see you and with your inner emotions and mental stories, is not conducive to communication with others. Externalize attention to extend interest in their direction rather than only desperately trying to get noticed. You give interest instead of trying to get it. You give an ear instead of seeking one. You lend a hand instead of needing one. Such attitude immediately turns the game-board around, making you source of goodwill and energy instead of its beggar.

Allowing yourself to flow a gentle state of Humor quickly dispels negative vibes, social masks and tension. "Flowing gentle Humor" does not mean cracking a joke every minute. It's an inner radiance. That radiance can be activated just by remembering to activate it. In a state of lightness it's easy to be authentic. You don't have to hide anything, scheme

anything, avoid anything, calculate advantages and disadvantages, imitate someone or be someone; you are just present with what is, here and now.
If the above statement is too long for you to remember, you could reduce it down to this shortcode: "You don't have to be anything, just BE".
From that basis, authenticity develops. From wearing no masks at all, being vulnerable and open, you also become free from the various social roles and masks usually played. From that basis you can create new ways-of-being, with the difference that these will be deliberately chosen rather than masks put on to please others. You are then real, honest, straightforward, daring to follow-your-bliss, daring to speak-up, not caught up in any inner story, daring to follow a unique lifestyle, daring to do what is right and true and congruent to you. How to know when you are not being authentic? When you are nervous. Your true self is never ill at ease. Only the Illusory-self is ill at ease.

A reason why some people suppress showing their true colors is because initially it makes them stand out. Someone who is shining brightly receives an inordinate amount of attention. Authenticity is a radical deviation from mediocrity as it may stir people up and you may not only get positive attention but also negative attention. So it's best to add a dash of humility to your overall being and habitually forgive those who envy or attack you.

Shameless

The word "shameless" has a negative undertone in most cultures, as its synonyms show: Improper, Brazen, Brash, Rude, Immodest, Unprincipled. I`d like to present the word in a more positive light. Clearing Shame – the lowest level on the Scale of Emotions. "Shamelessness" does not bring about being "brash, rude, immodest and unprincipled" but rather happy, bold and authentic. On a spectrum there is "Total Inhibition" at one end, and "Total Dis-Inhibition" on the other. Both are unhealthy extremes. However, the majority are too inhibited and timid to experience high energy success.

There is only a small group with too little inhibition: Criminals and the Ostentatious who trespass others boundaries without respect. The other day, exiting a train and walking through the station, I spotted a guy who was thrusting his fists into the face of a young lady…repeatedly! Here was a man who was clearly lacking in the shame/inhibition department. The inhibited majority passed by the scene actually looking down or away and it took security staff to restrain him. The girl was bleeding from her mouth and while the security officers dragged the man away, his facial expression still showed no sign of regret. But looking more deeply, we find that this kind of total dis-inhibition is not the opposite of inhibition but really the result of suppressed inhibition. Criminal shamelessness = suppressed shame. It`s a rebellion against shame, not freedom from it. Truly dis-inhibited people have no desire to provoke, physically confront, hurt, humiliate. The shameless state I am referring to is mostly harmless to oneself and others. Harmlessness goes hand in hand with a healthy psychology. But this doesn't't mean that a harmless person will not self-defend or intervene when outrageous injustices are witnessed. High consciousness is harmless in the sense that it will not attack – but it will defend.

There are three main drugs that suppress shame, making it appear as if a person were shameless: Alcohol and to a larger extent Cocaine and Amphetamines. If you have ever seen people on Cocaine you will notice that their shame seems to have been erased. They`ll talk and grin endlessly (to the annoyance of those who don't share their state), and generally behave as if they were invincible. An old trick used by the mafia to blackmail politicians, is to give them Cocaine and a Prostitute and then film them. Being thus dis-inhibited, the politician cares not about being filmed in the act, might even bask in the attention. Or a camera is secretly installed and he cares not to check. Later, they realize with shame and regret that someone now has the video that could ruin their career. The blackmailers then proceed to use his shame for extortion purposes.
In situations of war, where you need dis-inhibited, non-feeling soldiers you will always find a lot of speed and meth. Hitler himself was addicted to methamphetamine – and that is, in fact, the real fuel of his megalomaniac spree across Europe. All the modern armed conflicts you see in the news are also partially meth-driven. Without some altered-state that suppresses shame you couldn't harm others.

By contrast however, shame-suppression, the actual pockets of emotion and subconscious issues, are not really handled. If they were, the "shamelessness" would still be there after the drug-high recedes. The more suppressed shame there is, the more ostentatiously a person will act while high on drugs. So they don't do anything to handle the problem of low energy, they only perpetuate it. The brain is then led to believe that drugs are the "best way" to handle shame.

Positive shamelessness is a whole different ballgame. It's the conscious detecting, feeling and releasing of shame-emotions, leading to freedom from mental slavery, the reduction of excessive self-censorship, the letting go of "what do others think of me?"-fear. It is a fundamental component of successful and free living.

The "nice girl" and "nice boy" Identities we walk around with were formed in childhood. They are excessively concerned with wanting to make it right for others, pleasing others, never inconveniencing anyone, having false humility, being too quick to apologize (apology without examination), being ashamed of speaking up, being ashamed of standing ones ground, appeasing abusers, approval-seeking, or avoiding criticism.

"But isn't it good to want to look after others first and not always oneself?" you might ask. Well, note that I said "excessively pleasing others" in the paragraph above. Secondly, it depends on where your desire to look after others is coming from. It can come from a sense of submissive fear. One could also call it lack of a healthy Ego. Or it can come from a sense of freedom and confidence. In that case, then it's compassion or kindness. It`s important to differentiate here.

As taught in my book "Levels of Energy", before shedding the Ego, one should build the Ego. If a human being progresses on a scale from 1-10, then the levels 0-2 are ego-less, 3-6 gradually build up ones ego, character and personality and then from 7-10 one becomes Ego-less again. The high ego-less state is different than the low one. The low one is ego-less in the sense of having no opinion, no stance, no personality, no personal boundaries, no rights, no identity, no name, no reputation, no desires, or no goals. The high ego-less state is ego-less in the sense of being compassionate, kind, wise, free, untroubled, un-needy, etc.. At the bottom you give up your desires because you don't believe you can reach them. At the top you give up your desires because you have already reached them. Building a healthy and balanced Ego is a part of raising your Consciousness.

As children we asked "Who should I be and what should I do so that I am liked?" Changing our true heart to conform to others' expectations was a matter of survival. Then, in adulthood, we either carry that inauthentic and non-self-expressive self on, or we rebel against it by becoming "bad girl" and "bad boy" identities. The Higher Self is neither. It is neither "nice boy" (shame-based) nor "bad boy" (shame-suppression-based). It does not define itself through others' expectations but through its own choices.

In positive shamelessness you do not always have to

censor what you say, you can speak freely and spontaneously. The motivation to be liked and accepted (which paradoxically leads to you not being liked) is gradually replaced with the motivation to think, say and do what feels right and good to you. Imagine going on a blind date. Most people really believe they have to say, do or be something in order to make the other person "like you". The disinhibited self does not think it has to be anything. If you understand that, you will never feel uncomfortable with others again. There is nothing you have to say, do or be in order to "be liked". You can simply be whoever you are in that moment. You can say something but you do not have to. Your most natural self is effortless. And once you no longer resist who-you-are-now, guess what? It's easier to become a better-version-of-you. The motivation for becoming better is then internal, not external.

In your smiles and frowns you can easily see whether you are being the real you or whether you are living from a mask. Try this: If you do not feel like smiling, don't. If you do not feel like frowning, don't. Try to make your smiling or frowning or neutral-looking independent of others expectations and the surroundings. You do not "have to" smile just because someone else is and you are at their birthday party. Nor do you "have to" frown just because someone else is in a bad mood. This is an interesting exercise to learn about who-you-really-are vs. who-you-try-to-be-to-fit-in. Sure, sometimes when I don't feel like smiling I smile anyway, not to appease others, but in order to improve my own state. The difference lies in "where the smile is coming from", what motive underlies it.

Positive Shamelessness involves shedding shyness. Are you shy in front of certain people? Here's a quick exercise: Imagine the type of person you are shy in front of. Now imagine how they have bad breath and smell under the armpits. If that just made you laugh, then it's because the context was shifted from "they are above me" to "they are just human". In that instant, a big chunk of your shyness just fades away. You don't really need 6 years of therapy to "overcome shyness", all you need to do is fix your thinking.

Are you afraid of your upcoming interview on TV? Then imagine you have been doing these interviews for the past 10 years. Or the past 70 years. What does it feel like to have been doing them for 70 years? Painfully dull? That thought alone will reduce a large chunk of your anxiety.

Do you feel like you are a timid person? Then speak a little more loudly. Just that little shift will wipe out the timid-self within seconds.

Are you very clear toward others in saying what you want? Or do you hold back clarity for the sake of harmony? If so, you are creating the opposite of harmony. You are creating chaos. Harmony is created when you are clear with your thinking, feeling and speaking being aligned.

Setting your Boundaries

I was in the plane on an overseas flight recently. In

the aisle to my right were a husband and wife. The wife was angry during most of the flight and kept talking down to the guy. The guy was trying to please and appease her but she kept getting angrier, humiliating him in front of everyone. "Shut up you piece of shit!" she said for all to hear. He responded with "Darling, please keep your voice down" and she said "Why? Because you ask me to? You're an idiot. A loser! I told you to pack the perfume. You forgot. Admit that you're a piece of shit!" - "Honey, can we please discuss this later...." "Shut up you idiot!" It was an unpleasant sight to see someone publicly humiliated in this way.

What was going on here is that he hadn't set boundaries or lines that can't be crossed. "Public Humiliation" would seem to be "crossing the line" within healthy relationships. There were other seats free, he could have stood up and gone to another seat instead of taking that kind of abuse for what seemed like hours. If someone were to talk down to me like that, that's what I would have done. I´d say "Well, that's quite enough now honey. Bye!" If you have any self-respect, you won't just submit to unacceptable behavior. Because the guy hadn't set boundaries, I had to. I went over and said: "Ma'am, please be quiet, I'd like to read". Coming from a stranger, it impressed her and the rest of the flight she was quiet. Before that she had acted like the only person on the plane, with a complete disregard not only toward her husband but all other passengers in ears' length. From then on, all passengers had their peace. It wasn't easy for me to go over there and say that. Ten years ago I wouldn't have done it, I would have kept quiet as "not to rock the boat" but those little moments of authentic boundary-setting are invaluable tools for inner growth.

I could see that the guy was uncomfortable. His face had gone red with shame and guilt. My taking over and setting boundaries for him didn't help. The best thing he could have done in that situation, emotionally, was to release the shame and move up to the level of anger, and then move up even higher to a state of compassion...compassion for his stressed out wife. It was not him who should feel shameful, he wasn't the one shouting around. And then, to "regain face" he might have said something like "Sorry for all the commotion". But when you're wallowing in guilt, it's not that easy to come back up...guilt is low-density energy. Was guilt the appropriate reaction to having forgotten a flask of perfume and being humiliated for it? Hardly so.

Nonetheless, the actual problem will have started long before that. If the guy were to stop pleasing and appeasing her and instead set boundaries....would she leave him? Not likely. She`d respect him. Respect is not gained by trying to "do everything right" for another person. I am not advocating to do the opposite of that...of going around confronting people all the time. We would in this instance understand that the husband was going to the extreme of not confronting anything, and was greatly suffering for it. In an airplane, where he never sees the other people again, he can rehabilitate himself the moment he leaves the airport. What if he had been instead publicly humiliated in front of his friends or work colleagues? If he were my coachee we would start by talking about drawing lines and becoming crystal-clear about what is and is not appropriate. In more cases, if he has not drawn boundaries at home, he hasn't done so at work or other areas neither.

When you become authentic some people may not like that at first but in the long run they will feel more comfortable around you and even become attracted to you. It's much preferable to openly say "No" to someone or something than to pretend you are OK or friendly while harboring secret resentment. Hidden resentment silently eats away at so many relationships. Subconscious resentment builds when you say "Yes" when you really want to say "No". Saying "yes" when you mean otherwise, leaves the other person confused because mixed signals are being transported there. If you are not used to setting boundaries and saying "No" to what is not wholesome, then practicing it may take some courage at first. You might feel unwell about being clear but it's very much worth it to remain steadfast and to release those feelings of guilt. You do not have to apologize for being who you are and you do not have to be someone different than you are just to please others.

"But I want to be good to others! I want harmony". And I say: There is a difference between help coming from the heart and help coming from a sense of owing others something or wanting approval or expecting-something-in-return. "Compassion" that expects love or approval in return is not real compassion. That's why I teach that it's always a good idea to improve your own well-being first before trying to "fix" others. The best thing you can do for others is have a good state yourself. Looking at yourself first is not "selfish" but self-respecting. It is only when you have energy that you truly have something to give to others, that something not motivated by "wanting to please". Never be shy to openly state your preferences, desires and what is and is not good for you.

Where no boundaries are drawn, the misbehavior will happen again. I knew a lady who had an alternative healing practice in downtown. She was always making concessions, giving people free treatment, supposedly out of "good heartedness". The more free treatment she gave, the less people showed up. Finally she had to close her practice because she couldn't't pay the rent. The good-heartedness was fake. Its real motivation was fear of unworthiness. Accordingly, her clients did not think too highly of him so we worked on the idea of giving freely and generously...while also taking freely and generously. The "taking" part was what was missing in the equation. She then learned that she had a sense of shame about taking. Once that was overcome, her giving became more authentic. She then gave not to appease but out of joy. Soon her debts were paid off and she was back in Business.

Any reality you wish to create requires boundaries to be drawn. You must limit your focus to a particular frequency and reality and disregard anything that does not match what you have chosen. Saying "No" to a whole lot of things and "Yes" to the right things is the trademark of very successful people.

"If I am real and tell the truth, people won't like me", one guy said, but the truth is: You can't and shouldn't try to control whether someone likes you or not. Love yourself and treat yourself kindly and then some will like you and some won't. In either case, you will be easier to like, because you are happy.

"I have given him so much, why doesn't he love me?" one lady asked. The reason was: Because she wasn't really "giving", she was giving-and-expecting-love-in-return. See the difference?

"I did everything for her and now she left me for another guy. How is that possible?" another one asked. Well, you're doing everything for her probably has suffocated her, so she then left. She chose freedom over the butler. People don't want everything done for them, they want to develop on their own.

"I try to do everything right when raising my kids. Why won't they listen to me?" another one asked. It is because you cannot control others. Rather than trying to do "everything right" (=fear-based), be kind to yourself and release the perfectionism.

"He takes all of my money and spends it on drinking...but I forgive him, because I love him". Are you really sure you want him to waste the money you earned on his own self-destruction? Is that really love? Or would a "No" not be more loving toward both yourself and him?

In the last examples you can see how the words "everything" and "all" denote lack of boundaries. Your personal boundaries may be narrow or they may be broad, but they should be set. If they are not defined by you, others will define them for you, invade your space and use you as a doormat. Everyone has some of this "appeasing others" to some extent. Why? Because it was needed in childhood. "What must I do so that mommy and daddy like me?" was an important question back then. And we transfer that into adulthood by asking "What must I say and do so that people would like me?" The false conclusion being "If I do not set boundaries, people will like me". The opposite is true. When you say "No" or set boundaries you are helping people co-create reality with you because they learn the parameters and game rules within which a certain reality is experienced. Not doing so leaves people in a space of uncertainty, second-guessing, and confusion. You can start today by clearly defining what belongs in your life and what doesn't and then gradually getting rid of what doesn't…even if it appears painful at first. In the long run, it's not painful, it's liberating. If truth seems painful to you then it's long overdue to take your life back and re-discover that truth is wonderfully refreshing.

One more thing: If you don't want to ruffle too many feathers, note that setting boundaries does not require an angry or rigid tone. If done with fearless calm, your boundary-setting is more easily taken by others. Of course that doesn't guarantee that nobody will be offended. If you carry the torch of truth, some beards will be parched. You can minimize the turbulence by coming-from-calm.

Exercise: Say "no" to something you have been

wanting to say "no" to for some time.
Exercise: Tell the truth about something you have wanted to tell the truth about for some time, even if it's not easy.

Exercise: Say "yes" to something you have been wanting to say "yes" to for some time.

10 Factors that strengthen your Integrity

1. Shift from "what will I get?" to "what will I give?"
2. List your strengths and weaknesses and work to eradicate your weaknesses and train your strengths.
3. When you are saying "No" on the inside, do not say "Yes" on the outside. You can also say "No" gently.
4. Openly communicate the issues you see. Do not hide. Go where it hurts and change that to the positive.
5. Understand before wanting to be understood.
6. Interest in others makes you interesting.
7. Be more attentive with giving your word and your words in general.
8. Follow a vision higher than yourself.
9. Serve others without detriment to yourself.
10. Live from the context of your values and principles.

Being an Upright Person

You can be an upright person physically and psychologically/spiritually. One affects the other. An upright body posture improves your state and authority. If you have the habit of slumping or being unconscious in your physical movements you can gain a little extra power by correcting your posture. Depending on setting, you can also take in various deliberate poses. Stretching your arms to the sky, for example, creates an immediate openness for energy. Your mind acts according to your body movements. Having more control over your space will create that feeling in the mind. Tensing the muscles or crossing your arms tends to heighten concentration. Smiling deliberately tends to increase joy. Using gesture consciously tends to make it easier to persuade someone. The basis of conscious and deliberate movement is Uprightness. Being upright indicates that you are aware of what is happening around you. Uprightness is not very useful when you are sitting at home watching a movie, but it is useful when you have an important meeting. Uprightness is a matter of straightening your spine. It only takes a second of awareness. So that Uprightness does not become Uptightness, it is best alternated with phases of relaxing your posture.

Psychological Uprightness is your ability to remain loyal to your heart's path even in challenging and difficult situations. How easy would it be to distract you from a path you have chosen? Do you sway with the winds of change or do you keep firm in your values and principles? Are you easily swayed by fear and desire? Can you stick to your goal even if people say you should give up? Psychological Uprightness is resilience.

To be spiritually upright means to "have spine". When you "have spine" it means that you don't cave in at the slightest temptation or interruption. If I offer you $50 000 to betray your best friend (and he would never find out) and you refuse it out of a sense of integrity, it's because you "have spine". On a soul-level, nothing is hidden so even if you manage to hide things in the physical, you can't really ever hide something. That's why being of upright character is incredibly empowering. A lot of people who are looking for "magic" to fix things for them would be better served cultivating integrity and to thereby become integrated-beings. "To be integrated" means to act as a part of the whole, in respect toward the society one lives in.

How to Increase your Wordpower

So that your spoken word gains authority and power, reduce lying, chatter, gossip. If you tell a lie this, hurts you more than it hurts another. Why? Because you are teaching your subconscious that your word is of no consequence or reality. Hence, next time you want to use your word to create a reality, your intention will have no effect. After all, you have taught yourself that what you say is not true. If however you have conditioned your body/mind to believe that your word is true, then what you say will more easily manifest in your life. Affirmations, Prayers and Incantations only gain traction if your word has enough power. Ways to increase it:

1. Silence

A human has two ears and one mouth for a reason. This is nature telling you that the amount of listening should be double the amount of speaking. If you talk too much your word power is not conserved but dispersed. But then, when you finally do talk, your word will have much more weight. If you hold presentations, make several pauses throughout. It is in the empty spaces between talking that the attention of the audience is captured. The words then spoken have more impact than had you talked in one long never-ending ramble. Silence also allows you to gather your thoughts so that what finally comes out of your mouth sounds good. This rule does not apply to shy people who feign "Silence" because they are afraid to talk. If you are shy of speaking, do the opposite of what is recommended here so that your word begins having some impact.

2. Stop Gossip

Talking about others positively is energizing, but whenever possible avoid talking badly about others because this ultimately reflects badly upon you, not only on the people you are gossiping about. Most people are immediately game when someone starts gossiping, they love to hear it, but their subconscious-self is judging you for it. What they are really thinking is: "When I'm not around, they will be gossiping about me!" Gossip is one of the great energy wasters and thousands of magazines thrive on it, sucking in people's attention (= life energy). You do have the choice to turn away from gossip – your own and others. When I catch myself becoming curious about someone's misdeeds I usually stop myself. When I start ranting about other people, I usually stop myself and change the subject. When I become drawn into some newspaper article involving celebrity-gossip, I do my best to wake up and stop reading.

3. Keep your word

Breaking your promises or intentions has the most crippling effect on your wordpower because you are teaching yourself that what you say does not come true. You can refine the skill of keeping your word even to the smallest detail: If you say you are going to meet someone at 8 o'clock, then do your very best to show up at 8 o'clock. Your subconscious takes note of such details and assumes that your word is worth something. You can't be lying and speaking untruth and then later in the day expect your Intentions to come true. Just to "make an impression" we sometimes promise things we have no real intention of keeping. It's best not to promise too much if you are not sure about it. Of course "I would like to make it at 8 o'clock" does not sound as firm as "I´ll be there at 8", but sometimes it's the better choice of words.

4. Do a Vocabulary Makeover

Learn new Vocabulary and new non-routine ways of expressing yourself. Also notice how what words people use reveals a lot about their intentions and their current state. There is a big difference whether you start the day by saying "Fuck, I missed the goddamn train" or you start it by saying "I thank the most High for a miraculous day ahead". Your spoken word is a bolt of energy that leaves your body the moment you speak it. It goes out into the Universe.

And it returns to you. The other day I heard someone use the word "Awesomeness". I had never used that word before so I decided to apply it that day. Learning new words to use keeps your mind and speech fresh and light.

5. Speak words of Appreciation

Get into the habit of praising things and people. Bestow your words of blessing and appreciation everywhere you go. Do not do this to manipulate people or when you don't mean it. But when you do mean it, express it. There are waiters, cab drivers, spouses, bosses, employees, friends out there who will immediately lighten up when you find something about them to appreciate. But the real secret is that it benefits you even more than it benefits them.

Don't trust the Alarmist

An alarmist is someone who grossly exaggerates a threat to mankind, a region, a person or to themselves. You also have an inner alarmist who goes by the name of fear, and several external alarmist who are trying to convince you that things are not well and going downhill fast.

I don't trust alarmists and remain unresponsive to them. Here's a sampling of a few alarmist-statements that have been carried to me in the last decade which I failed to respond to in any way:

"The swine flu is going to wipe out civilization as we know it. You better be sure and you better be prepared. Stock up and shut yourself out before it's too late!!!!!"

Response: No. Not going to happen.

"We are living in the greatest economic depression the country has ever seen. It's time to stock up on foods because the end is nigh!"

Response: Back in the late 1930s they lined up to get a loaf of bread – if they were lucky. Today they line up to get the latest i-pad. I don't think we have the same definition of economic depression.

"The President is going to implement a nationwide dictatorship! Better plan your escape ASAP!!!!!"

Response: Not going to happen.

"Oh my God! You have coding errors on your website! Google will down-rank you and you will lose customers because of it!!!!!"

My Response: I`m no slave of Google. The source of my Abundance is the Infinite Universe, not Google.

Alarmists are attention-seekers who exaggerate a threat to gain someone's ear or induce worry. Some alarmists are stealth-marketers who want to sell you something. Where there is an alarmist there is usually a liar. Even if something bad is happening, that would be no reason to talk about it in a crazed, sensationalist tone. Fear would not help a bad situation anyway, only action would. The point I am making is: Do not allow alarmists to create a state of fear for you. Even if the world were to explode, your soul lives on. Integrity means to provide positive information to others. If positive information cannot be provided, then at least provide accurate, non-generalizing, non-overhyped information.

The End of Grovelling

Grovelling is harmful to your integrity. A few synonyms to illustrate in which sense I mean the word:

Needy, beggarly, servile, boot-licking, obsequious, slavish, submissive, false humbleness, spineless, cringing, squirming, craving, longing, destitute. And a few antonym to make the point clearer: Worthy, noble, royal, abundant, proud, exalted, excellent, bold, cool, unyielding, respectable, commendable, upright.

A few examples of grovelling I've witnessed in real life:

* A woman wants a big-name Hollywood producer to read her film-script so she works for two years in his office getting his coffee, washing his car, babysitting his kids, telling lies for him and even having sex with him any time he commands. And all this with the vague promise that he might "someday" read her script (and just read it, not even approve of it). Of course, because she has completely compromised her integrity, she will never succeed. It much later turns out he never bothered to read it, it had been thrown

in the garbage long before.

* A guy wants to marry a specific woman, his "dream woman" as he says. Before even getting to first base she has him pay for her vacation. On vacation she says she wants to go jet-skiing, so he arranges it. Shortly before the appointment, she says she has changed her mind and would rather go on a yacht, so he says "of course!" and arranges for it. She fails to show up at the arranged time and instead joins a beach party elsewhere. When she comes back he does not confront her about it or demand an apology. This goes on for another week with him never ever saying "no" to any of her antics and agreeing to everything she wants. Naturally, she gets incredibly bored with this spineless wimp and kicks him to the curb. He is "heartbroken" and says "I don't understand how she could leave me! I did everything for her!" But that's exactly the problem buddy…you did everything for her, regardless of whether it violated your sense of value, principle, truth or respect. You can't possibly be interesting to her in such a submissive state.

In a state of grovelling you are profoundly out of touch with your internal abundance. You instead project too much importance into other people, bosses, superiors, celebrities, VIPs. When around them your attention becomes locked and frozen on them, not noticing or perceiving or even being interested in anything other than them and making a "good impression". Self-confidence is the polar opposite of that. Your internal world is sufficient onto itself. You appreciate others' attention, but if they don't give it to you, you think "that's their loss, not mine". Or you don't think anything at all. No human being is more important than the Infinite and

Eternal Being of which you are a miniature-version. The person of Integrity waits not for the bosses email, for the client's praise, for the bank's money, for the world's applause, the partner's attention, the VIP's recognition or Google's ranking. He or she waits for nothing and nobody because he/she is brimming with energy and joy in the here and now.

Walk Away or Try Harder?

A typical dilemma many face when in an uncomfortable situation is whether they should try to improve it or focus elsewhere. "Should I stay in my troubled relationship and try to make it better or should I let go of it and look elsewhere?" "Should I hold on to my Business that isn't working or should I let go and become open for something better?" people ask me. I don't have a simple answer for this dilemma but I can assure you that both paths have merit. Walking away is the practice of letting go of unnecessary baggage. Trying harder is the practice of making yourself stronger to carry the baggage. If you drop the baggage you feel lighter. If you keep the baggage you will become stronger. I'll usually tell people that life can be a fluid and balanced mix of both modes of behavior. You wouldn't walk away every time the going gets a little tough. But neither would you put up with years of trouble. Knowing that both paths have merit and advantages makes the decision less hard.

4
How to Stop Fear

Fear is the magnet that draws strange undesirable stuff into your life. It`s sisters are shyness, paranoia, timidity, panic and worry. It shows up as fear of rejection, fear of job loss, fear of partner loss, fear of financial ruin, fear of being in the spotlight, phobia of closed spaces, phobia of insects, phobia of open spaces, fear of oblivion, fear of aging, fear of loneliness, fear of heights, fear of noise, fear of the unknown…the list is endless.

Neurotic vs. Natural Fear

My estimate is that 95% of all fears are neurotic or subjective and only 5% are natural or legitimate protections of danger. They feel different too. An example of a healthy and positive fear: The fear of poisonous snakes. That fear helps you make a detour around the danger instead of walking into your physical death. However, even this fear can become neurotic and subjective when even the sight of a snake behind safe glass makes you freeze or when you are paranoid about snakes in your bedroom where there are none. Items where neurotic and natural fears are mixed are the most difficult to overcome because people have a hard time differentiating. Another example for this is the fear of heights. It is natural to be skeptical of heights as not to plummet off a skyscraper while on visit with your kids. But it's neurotic to have so much fear that even despite the fenced wall you become sick and dizzy at certain heights. Here we are talking about neurotic fears, which make up the majority. It goes without saying that you don't have to go to therapy to get rid of your fear of poisonous snakes or rapid machine gun fire when and if they are nearby or on their way. Instead of going to therapy, get out of the way of the rapid fire!

Why suppressing fear wastes life energy

When a fear keeps recurring we tend to suppress it because we can't stand it anymore. Let's say there is an exam in two weeks and you are terrified because you haven't really studied for it. So if instead of handling the fear by either changing your thoughts (beliefs) about the exam or your actions (more study) toward the exam you go ahead and ignore it (suppress it), you will start feeling exhausted or get a headache. The fear won't be as intense anymore but you will also be feeling less lively. The following image clarifies the idea:

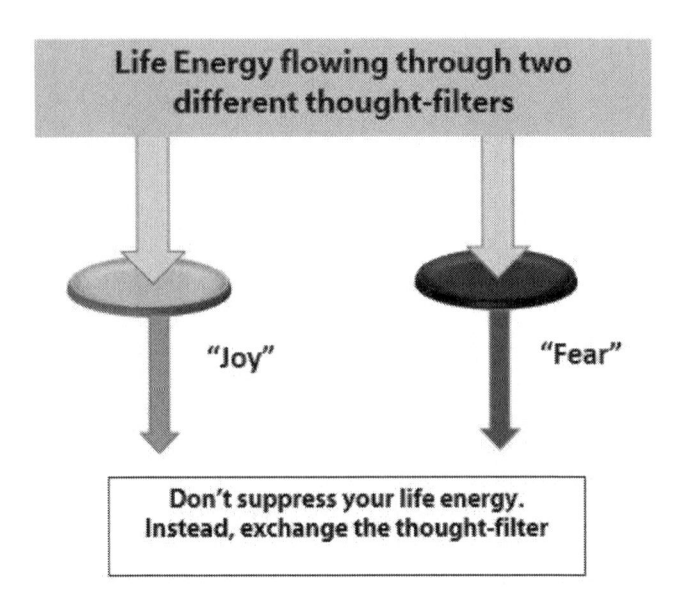

Life Energy flowing through two different thought-filters

"Joy" "Fear"

Don't suppress your life energy.
Instead, exchange the thought-filter

Fear and Joy

In this sense, love, joy, fear, hate are all the "same energy" flowing through different filters (beliefs / thoughts). If you suppress the emotion or sensation of fear, you are suppressing life energy, hence the tiredness, hence the headache, hence the fear continuing to cry out from the subconscious. I have found that this spiritual understanding of fear has a positive impact on anyone who has learned it. It's a game changer. You can derive from it that the question "How do I get rid of the fear?" is the wrong one. The right one is: "What thought is creating this sensation?" It`s the dirty filter you want to change, not the water that runs through it. So coming back to the exam in two weeks, the answer might be: "The thoughts I have about this are that I don't know enough". So I ask: And what happens if you don't know enough?" and you say "I fail". And I ask: "And what happens if you fail?" and you say: "My parents will see me as a failure and I won't get a job". This style of questioning leads to deeper seated thoughts, until we find the one that is creating the fear feeling. Once the fear thought is discovered, it needs to be replaced with a better filter. This new thought must be close enough to home or realistic enough to be instantly feel-able. So if we replace it with "My parents will be happy if I fail", that might work temporarily and bring out a laugh, but I'm not sure this thought will "stick". A better thought might be: "I believe that if I study with a little more interest and dedication, I can pass the exam. And even if I don't I could repeat it. I can do my best and then we'll see. Whether I make it or not, I have enough self-respect not to worry about things that haven't happened yet. Now let's get to work". Once you have found a thought that is realistic and "feels just right" you run it by your mind a few times, getting used to it. The reason for this is so that you can revert back to it later just in case you relapse into the old thought. And with just a little practice you will have overcome your fear and feel entirely different.

If relapse into the old pattern comes too easily, there is still some work to do. You then run the old thought a few more times or question whether there is yet another thought behind the already discovered one. Then you go back to running the new thought. In time, detecting and replacing fear-thoughts becomes second nature and happens within a minute. I became aware of this way of seeing fear about 20 years ago and today it takes only a few seconds to drop the old filter and re-phrase my thinking to something that feels better. So rather than suppressing fear, I know to handle it and life is good.

A quick and intense alternative approach

An alternative quicker approach that does not involve a number of thought-shifting sessions is to simply face, confront and go through what you fear. It is based on the principle "Courage is not the absence of fear, it's moving forward in spite of fear". Doing so, of course, disappears the fear rather rapidly. Whatever you are worried about, go straight toward it instead of away. Instead of holding your breathe, breathe it in. The way out is the way through. If you're only shying away from fear because you want to feel comfortable all the time, you will never feel the energy that is so much stronger and better than merely "feeling comfortable". You`ll be feeling fantastic.
With this method, you put yourself into the situations you were afraid of, until you can handle them with ease. Not the situations that threaten your survival but the harmless things – such as public speaking, confessing something to a relative, proposing to someone, etc. You use this on fears that are stopping you to live fully. Are you afraid of failing? Then go out and try to fail deliberately a few times. Embrace failing. Fail! It's not as bad as the mind thinks it is. You are not the mind, you are not the body, so it's not really YOU that is failing. Anyone who has

achieved Greatness had to fail a hundred times before achievement. It is not the Failure that is ruining your life, it is the fear of failure, the frozenness you get when you don't want to act because you are afraid you will fail. People who never fail are usually not succeeding either.

Are you afraid of rejection? Then go out and try to get rejected several times. Get rejected so often that it gets boring. You will discover that you can't really be "rejected" unless you have not rejected yourself first. By putting yourself into the position you were most afraid of and staying poised and accepting during that situation, you overcome fear of rejection.

Are you afraid of a certain person? Strike up a conversation with them. In 9 cases out of 10 you will notice that your fears were unfounded and that the mind was only projecting that that person is "very important". When you approach the person they will either turn out to be more friendly than you thought, or not so friendly. And if they are not so friendly – who cares? That is not your problem, it's theirs. You don't require everyone to be friendly or in agreement with you, do you? You're not a child.

Are you afraid of losing your assets? Then let me tell you this: Many of richest self-made Millionaires have lost all of their money several times. That's what made them free. They had no fear of losing it all which is why they gained it all. Did you know that an above-average amount of self-made millionaires don't come from the middle-class but from the lower-classes of society? Do you know why that is? It's because they are hungrier. But it's also because, already having hit rock bottom, they are no longer afraid of it. When you lose everything, you have everything to gain.

Are you afraid of losing your spouse? If that's what you are afraid of….that's what will happen! Fear tends to attract what it is afraid of. So either let go of your fear or allow it to happen. Once you authentically allow it to happen…you may find that it does not happen.

And to make all this easier on you: Sometimes it's enough to imagine doing these things and to embrace them fully to overcome the fear.

Releasing the Fear of Death

Behind many secondary fears there is the primary fear of Death. Overcome the Fear of Death and the lesser Fears fall away too.
My favorite fear-questioning technique is:

1. What are you afraid of?
2. And what if that happens?
3. And what if that happens (regarding the answer to the last question)?
4. Etc.

As you take this technique to its core you usually end up with death, oblivion, extinction, eternal imprisonment or some other such nonsense. The technique can be taken to its extreme, until it becomes kind of silly. Here's an example (this is from an original coaching transcript I did with a student some years ago):

1. What are you afraid of?
"Losing the job"
2. And what if that happens?
"Then I won't be able to pay the rent and provide for my family"
3. And what if that happens?
"Then they will see me as a loser and we will be unhappy"
4. And what if that happens?
"Then I will be separated from my family and become homeless".
5. And what if that happens?
"I will be in a dark and lonely place"
6. And what if that happens?
"I don't know"
7. Think about it. What then?
"Then I will starve or freeze to death"
8. And what if that happens?
"Nothing. I will be dead"
9. But what might happen then? Suppose there is an afterlife.
"Then I will be punished for failing"
10. What kind of punishment?
"Maybe I'll be damned to a dark place. Or I'll have to reincarnate as an insect"
11. And what if that happens?
"If I come back as an insect, I'll be squashed"
12. And what if that happens?
"I'll die again"
13. And what if that happens? Speculate. What's the worst thing that could happen?

"I'll go to hell"
14. And what if that happens?
"I'll be tortured in hell"
15. And what if that happens?
"I'll be tortured some more. Forever"
16. And what if that happens?
"I'll be tortured so much I won't even exist anymore"
17. And what if that happens?
"I will cease to exist"
18. And what if that happens?
"Nothing"
By this time the student had a huge grin on his face. It was starting to get ridiculous. So I added:
"So all this worry about losing your job…is over NOTHING?"

If you keep up with the inquiry you will almost always find that it leads to death or extinction and then behind that…to nothing. The process is done until the person feels well. The reason he feels well is because he has been through it all, confronted it all and has nothing more to lose. You also get a sense of the truth of your existence, which is: You cannot be extinct. And even if you could, it wouldn't matter because you wouldn't know because you are extinct!

Familiarity reduces Fear

The first time I went out with a girl at the age of 15 I was terrified. Her looks, the way she smelled, talked and acted had me anticipating the event over and over in my mind many days before we even met. Often the anticipated is more terrifying or joyful than the actual event. Anyway, despite thinking I was "lucky" to go out with her I was miserable. The meeting was awkward because I was constantly in Thinking-Mode (over-thinking is an attempt to cover-up fear). Suppressing the fear to the extreme in order to make a "good impression" for the short time we were together, I felt drained afterwards. The Delusion of shyness comes from the false idea that the other person is constantly judging or scrutinizing you. This, in turn, is connected to too much thinking about how one appears to the other. It's the inner-child seeking approval. Of course my own discomfort radiated out to her, making her feel uncomfortable as well, which is why we agreed to meet "another time".

I was lucky we even met again considering how uncomfortable I had made her feel. The second time we met, there was some familiarity and I actually began noticing her shortcomings. In the grip of terror I hadn't noticed them before. And with noticing more I realized I did't have to be quite as scared as I was. The third time we met I began enjoying myself. We got closer. Familiarity lessened the fear. Anything and anyone you put your attention on for a while, you gradually resonate with. With familiarity, fear decreases. We were now able to actually authentically laugh for the first time. And now that the fear was almost entirely gone I noticed…HER FEAR! My fear then quickly subsided and turned into COMPASSION…and the desire to help her feel comfortable. How preoccupied had I been at the first meeting not to have noticed her discomfort?

I tell you this story so that you have a basic understanding of how to overcome fear. The key is awareness, familiarity and courage. You fear only what you are unfamiliar with or feel unable to handle.

Hence the first meeting with anyone may be a little tense but with more time spent with the person, things begin to relax. The reason people like to take a glass of wine or beer with each other is in order to skip the process of gradually easing up. But similar can also be accomplished by deliberate relaxing. Overcoming the Fear of Death then, follows the same process. As you familiarize yourself with peoples tales of near-death-experience or those who passed away peacefully (for example), you relax on the subject. All Phobias are essentially fear of Death. By more closely examining that which you are afraid of, while reducing resistance, the fear turns into a sense of peace.

Overcoming Stage Fright

If you are a singer, artist, speaker who performs in front of large audiences and you experience stage fright, you can overcome this by no longer splitting your attention into past and future. Concerning yourself with whether you prepared (attention on past), what the audience will think (attention on future) or resisting failure (attention on past and future + resistance) is certain to create unnatural tension. If your stage-fright is high you will, in the beginning, have to invest some extra effort to keep your attention on your present surroundings. The whole idea of stage fright is from the inner child that is seeking approval from the audience. So it is best not to have your attention on how you look or what others think but single-pointedly on the overall space you are in (the room) or on the audience or on your upcoming performance. No matter where you put your attention, you will have to move it there deliberately and invest effort to keep it there. As you do so, your attention no longer splits into several branches and energy and calm are preserved. Go on stage in slow and deliberate movements. Connect your heart to your audience. Remain aware of the space you are in. Breathe slowly and deeply. Repeat this conscious and deliberate poise until you are in control of the space you are in. Before each entry to the stage, make the strong and unbending intention to maintain poise.

That's one approach to take. Another approach is to address the root cause of stage-fright which is childhood-based addiction to approval and fear of disapproval. To transcend the same, you would meditate as follows:

a) Imagine getting disapproval (being rejected)
B) Imagine getting approval

Alternate between these two states at least a dozen times, back and forth, until you can embrace both not getting approval and getting approval, not getting praise and getting praise, not being loved and being loved. Once you can view either side with equanimity, you have transmuted the energy stuck in it - and that's something big that few people ever achieve. They might go through years of psychotherapy addressing the surface of this but you can fix it in a few dedicated Meditation sessions.

Of course there are other methods to handle stage fright, such as imagining that the room you are in is empty or that the audience is sitting there nude or imagining yourself into a better state, but these are temporary methods that don't address the core issues. They will work in cases of emergency, but the problem will keep reemerging until it is transcended. Normally, stage fright recedes with practice. Having done more than a thousand workshops in front of groups I no longer feel any tension when standing there performing. Even unfamiliar and unexpected situations don't bother me. That's the value of repetition and practice. Being confident about what you do will significantly reduce your anxiety. Applying all three ideas you would therefore repeat the following process:

a) Improve your skill
b) Be OK with disapproval and approval
c) Become fully present, deliberate and single-pointed on stage

How to feel at ease in social situations

For those who have felt unwell among others, among friends and strangers, among superiors and employees the key to all of it lies in your reactive-ness. What is it you are reacting to you? You are reacting to what you think others expect of you. The mix of your own expectations and the expectations you think they have creates tension. In being different than you actually are, you begin feeling shy and just wanting to go home where you can again "be yourself".
The next time you are in a social situation with others or in some business meeting, slow down and become present. Become fully aware of what is happening right now. Reduce your reaction. Softly extend your

attention to others with no pressure to say or do anything. So rather than thinking "What should I say now?" or "What should I do to show how nice I am?" or "What do others think of me?" or "What do I think of them?" or "Where would I rather be", you gently give awareness the present surroundings with zero expectation. Relax. From presence, ease arises where your speaking becomes more spontaneous (not pre-defined, pre-pared, pre-parsed or calculated). In fact, from this state, things you say can be quite humorous and insightful. When someone addresses you or asks you a question, do not feel that you "have to" react immediately. Take a breathe before responding. Leave some silence between your words. Make eye contact before speaking. As you slow down the entire process of communication you regain control of the entire situation. Your communication becomes more thoughtful and listeners more attentive. Here's a secret: If you yourself actively listen to people you will come across as an "interesting person" even if you don't say anything all evening. When showing up in a professional situation (job interview, business meeting, etc.), remember that you are not a beggar, you are a provider of service. Think of yourself as someone who has valuable things to give instead of one who is lacking value and looking for it.

Your experience of social situations will undergo a remarkable shift when you first cut down on reactive-ness, then increase present-moment awareness, make pauses in your speaking (which captures listeners attention) and practice active listening. If you were socially inept up to now you can drop all of that within only a few practice rounds.

Less self-importance, more self-confidence

Your self-confidence increases with a lessening of your self-importance. What it first sight may seem like a paradoxical statement, makes more sense when you understand the so-called "Spotlight Effect". To quote from the Encyclopedia:

"The spotlight effect is a common form of social anxiety that causes people to have a tendency to overestimate the extent to which surrounding others notice aspects of one's appearance or behavior, and the extent to which they are aware of it. The spotlight effect can lead people to feelings of paranoia and self-doubt. This also makes people believe that they will be judged harshly based on their failures. Overall, the spotlight effect explains how people overestimate the amount of attention that is focused on them in group settings. The importance of the spotlight effect is that it allows people to understand that even during embarrassing moments, others around them are not judging their actions as harshly as they think they are. Eventually when people start to understand the concept of this phenomenon, they will feel more comfortable with themselves when they are caught in a blunder surrounded by people".

In other words, you are just not that important to others. They are mostly preoccupied with themselves, not with you. Believing that people are considering you and judging you all the time, will have you feel self-conscious. Understanding that people have a short memory-span as well, means they likely won't remember little "mistakes" you make either.

I have been coaching people in public speech and presentation for 20 years now, and communicating this basic principle to them has gone a long way in alleviating feelings of insecurity. "Suppose nobody gives a damn, nobody notices and nobody remembers?" I`ll ask. "Then I would be free!" they`ll respond. The essential trick is to reverse attention. Rather than asking "How do I look?" and "What do they think of me?" and "How can I make a good impression?" I ask: How do they look? What do I think of them? Are they making a good impression? This instantly alleviates any sort of shyness as it is not I that is the center of attention. In difficult negotiations, job interviews and business settings this principle is applied by asking the other questions, letting them do the talking.

You will notice that high self-importance and arrogance go hand in hand with sheepishness and shyness. So someone who is very arrogant in one situation, may suddenly become very sheepish when encountering someone he deems "above" himself. The strong polarization in "above and below", the exaggeration of the rank and status idea is what causes this kind of timidity. The person is constantly comparing himself to others, as to whether he is "higher" or "lower". When he encounters someone supposedly "lower" he is arrogant, with someone "higher" he is shy. When you are living from the heart, such silly considerations vanish. That's not to say that statuses and ranks don't exist, but they are no longer a preoccupation or cause of fear. When you feel comfortable with yourself, then you also feel comfortable with anyone else - the rich, poor, smart, good, bad, ugly, strong, silly, weak, pretty, crazy, small crowds, large crowds, women, men, children, old people, parents, bosses, employees, whoever. Unless someone has an extremely negative aura, it's fairly easy to feel comfortable in almost any social setting when you stop projecting.

5
Communication Excellence

This chapter presents simple pointers that will further refine your Communication.

People I like and dislike

Using a separate sheet of paper, list some people you dislike, along with the traits you dislike about them. After that, check if you have had similar traits sometimes. If so, write that trait down. If not, then don't write anything. If for example you dislike the trait "stubborn" about someone and you find you are sometimes pretty stubborn yourself, you would have the word stubborn in both columns ("Traits I dislike" and "My similarities"). Some of the traits you dislike are projections of what you don't like about yourself. After that, write down something you respect about each of these people. Even if it's difficult, try to find something. Radiating some respect towards all will keep your friends close and your enemies at bay. What you radiate out into the world is what you ultimately get back. Finally, write down what your Intentions are regarding your future Communication with them.

Examples for Intentions:

I'd like them to listen to me more carefully
I'd like more honesty between us
I'd prefer to feel neutral towards them
I'd prefer a friendly relationship with them
I'd like them to participate in the project

Simply define what it is you'd prefer. If you keep defining what you don't want and don't like, you will keep getting stuff you don't want and don't like. If you don't define anything at all, what you get will remain random. So make it an official exercise to keep stating your actual intentions regarding a thing. You might not always get what you intend, but you do increase the likelihood of it happening when you shift what you are looking for. So on your separate sheet of paper your table would include this:

People I dislike
Their traits I dislike
Similar traits I have
What I do respect about these people
My intentions regarding my Communication with them

After you are finished, list people you like, the traits you like about them, your similarities and finally your Intentions regarding Communications with them. Do not assume that it is always easier to Communicate with people you like – sometimes it's harder because the interaction lacks neutrality or because you might be looking up to them. Both too much "looking down at" and too much "looking up at" can inhibit free flow of Communication. So include Intentions that would improve your experience with them. On your separate sheet of paper your items would be:

People I like
Traits I like about them
My similarities
My intentions regarding Communication with them

Having completed it all: What do you conclude from this exercise? Have you experienced a change of state or attitude? Do you feel lighter? Did you have a new realization? Please write down what you feel still needs some practicing in the days to come in order to integrate this lesson into daily life.

Communication Disturbances

The disturbers of good Communication flow:

Environmental (such as loud music or drilling)
Physiological (such as deafness or blindness)
Semantic (such as a different interpretation of what a word means)
Syntactical (Mistakes in Grammar, Verbs, Tenses)
Organizational (poor structure of thoughts, unclearness, confusion)
Cultural (coming from ignorance of others customs, values and beliefs)
Psychological (unresolved emotional issues and projections coming into play)

Semantic, Organizational and Psychological issues often go unnoticed and cause more Communication Problems than Environmental or Physiological issues which are easily recognized and therefore easily changed.

The exercise here is to write down examples where these disturbers came into play in your own life or with people you know. The more examples you become aware of the more likely it is you notice them in daily life and can avoid them by recognition.

Acknowledgment

People naturally need approval and acknowledgment. Too much acknowledgment appears strange but the most frequently made mistake is giving too little acknowledgment. It is important to acknowledge what someone said or to acknowledge that you understand what someone said. Acknowledgment is the lubricant that keeps Communication flowing. It does not always mean that you agree but it does mean that you received the message or understand what was said. People who forget to give acknowledgment are often perceived as ego-centric, impolite, needy or lost in thought.

Examples for Acknowledgement:

A nod
A paraphrase
"Yes"
"OK"
"Alright"
"I see"
"I received your message"
"Thanks for your message"

Exercise: In order to commit this to memory, take a day or two in which you exaggerate the giving of nods, acknowledgement, "yes" and "OK's" to everyone along your way. Acknowledgement given will improve the way others perceive you.

Communication flow

One way to improve your Communication flow with someone is to find things you and the other agree upon. This will quickly increase the "vibe" you have with each other. Salespeople misuse this by pretending to be in Agreement on several issues with people they want to sell to. But people are smart and I recommend you find things you actually agree on with the other (if you want to improve your Communications with them).

Another way to improve your Communication flow is by Appreciation. For example, you could find out things you like about the person. This will shift your attitude and ultimately increase your positive "vibe" with the other.

Of course simply talking to them more often can increase your rapport, but it is always much easier if Appreciation and Agreement are added.
If you disagree with too many people or dislike too many people you will generally feel more "low" and weak in life.

The solution is to either reduce your aversion towards people you dislike or find more people you do like to hang out with. Love them or Leave them.

Approval and Disapproval

This is a guided Meditation you best let someone else speak while you mentally and emotionally go through the process. Alternatively you can also read it to yourself.

Who did you want approval from?

Could you relax needing/lacking approval from that person a bit?

Imagine having approval from that person.

Relax.

Who wanted approval from you?

Could you relax resisting giving approval a bit?

Imagine giving approval.

Relax.

Repeat dozens of times with the same person or other people, until the neediness of approval is relaxed and the resistance toward giving approval is eased.

Physical Movement

Communication is also physical movement. Have you ever moved an elbow only to have them move theirs too? If when you move they move too, that is an indicator that their attention is with you. If in a group someone has their foot directed at you it is often an indicator that their attention is on you. Gestures and Facial Expressions have the power to underline and emphasize your words or to properly express agreement and disagreement.

An interesting exercise I have used in Communication Courses is to watch people negotiating on Video without Sound. Then I ask: Who is in Command? You don't need to hear the words, it's enough to see the physical behavior.

Another exercise I often use is to have people Communicate without speaking until the other understands what is being communicated. An extension of that is to practice being in Command without talking – by mere posture and presence. The big lesson here is that you do not have to speak to be in Command of a situation. A few good examples of this are Al Pacino in "The Godfather" movies or Clint Eastwood in the 1970s western movies. They didn't have that much to say and yet – they were in command of themselves and therefore in command of the situation.

Posture and Position

There are postures which put you in Command and postures which put others in Command, depending on your Intention. Your lying down on a sofa is a relaxed posture while standing erect and your legs apart and firmly rooted in the floor is a more commanding posture. Changing your posture will always change the roles of an interaction.
The distance you are standing from someone, from where you are communicating, from which angle or location also have some influence. These parameters can also be changed depending upon what you wish to achieve. For example if you want more authority over a group, never sit with them in a circle but

instead with you in the front and perhaps even up higher or behind a podium. If on the other hand you wish to be friends and feel close to them, sit in a circle. Or if you wish to close an important deal it is preferable to do so in person than wanting to do it by email.

A note on touch: A handshake, a clap on the shoulders, a "coincidental" brush of the hands – all these are forms of Communication, as is lack of touch. The way you touch other objects than the person also says more about you than you may be aware of. If for example you are in a flirt-situation or on a date with someone, the way you handle her coat or his car-door may be taken as a hint on how you will handle him or her.

Look and Listen

It makes a difference whether you are looking straight at your partner, into his eyes, his face, between his eyebrows, to his sides or away and elsewhere. Depending on what you intend you can change the entire meaning of the Communication with where you look.

People can also sense whether you are listening or not. Active listening means that you are fully there without the need of speaking yourself. Active listening also means that you are thinking about what is being said. Passive listening is hearing the sounds but not really processing all that is said. With people we have an aversion towards, we listen passively; with people we like we or that have something interesting to say, we listen actively. I recommend you seek to understand before you wish to be understood. Communication is not only what you say but also what you don't say, withhold or fail to say. If for example you wish to retain power, speak less, chatter less, justify less, react less. If you do not want a situation to get out of hand, save your disagreement for a later time when you are in a better state. Such small feats of self-control can go a long way in succeeding in various venues. On the other hand, failing to communicate when it is necessary is not only an advantage it can also be a problem. Your motto should be "When uncertain, in doubt or in trouble, Communicate!" Half of all corporate problems are due to a lack of Communication and Clarity.

Reality Frames

Be respectful of others' limits and reality-frames. Peace and Harmony are just as much an asset as Truth and Frankness. Sometimes it is wiser to withhold comment for the sake of peace than to create turbulence where none is necessary. Many people are not mature enough to accept truth at all times and in all situations. Social Sensitivity is also about the Timing in which certain truths are shared. It is not necessary to "talk turkey about the struggling Business" while at a Funeral. In this case Peace and Harmony should be preferred to truth. Likewise it is not necessary to "be nice and calm" while Millions are being lost to mismanagement. In this case Truth and Frankness should be preferred to Peace and Harmony. Social Sensitivity is to behave respectful enough as to choose the right Timing and Situation for various Communications. When your employee calls off sick, don't have an assignment be your first Communication toward him and don't call at midnight. If you need to criticize your spouse, wait for the right moment. Don't do it while he is hurt or helping you with something.

To explore reality frames a little…

Write down something you think is true and others also think is true
Write down something you think is true and others think is not true
Write down something you think is not true and others think is true
Write down something you think is not true and others also think is not true

What conclusions do you draw from this?

Something that is true for everyone is called facts or Absolute Truth.

Something that is only true for some is called opinions or Relative Truth.

Mistaking the two is the cause of many problems. In regards to facts I recommend zero tolerance toward deviations and with regards to opinions full tolerance toward deviations from your opinion. But first learn to discern the two.

More on non-verbal Communication

An ancient Chinese saying goes: "If you want to enforce your will, speak softly". That means that disagreement can be expressed in an agreeable manner and that will more likely have the other respect your decision than if you try to force-feed your point with anger. Mood and Intention are the carrier-waves of words. You will get back what you put out. So if you say friendly words but have a bad vibe, bad vibe will come back. And if you say "no" but with positive vibe, positive vibe will come back. Saying "No" is not a problem. You can "let people have it your way" if you radiate good energy.
What you say is only 25% of the Information transmitted. How you say it is the other 75%. Who is the person saying it? What is his intention? Context is more important than Content.

What if you could read everyone's thoughts? Would you really want to?

I believe that you can read thoughts but have repressed the ability for two reasons: Firstly, you felt overwhelmed at the onslaught of all the neurotic thinking happening around you, secondly you did not want to open because it would mean others could read your thoughts too. You are then sitting at the table and you sense people thinking:

"He's stupid"
"How do I look?"
"Why is he looking at her?"
"Will he like me?"

"What does he think of me?"
"What an asshole"
"When will I be promoted?"
"Am I wasting my time?"
"These are nice people"
"Who am I?"
"Do they notice?"
"I need to say the right thing"
"I wish I could have him"
"I'm the best"
"I'm better than them"
"This should be interesting"

Most communication is non-verbal. That's a fact. What many haven't figured out yet but will in the future, is that none of this non-verbal communication is actually hidden. Even if you repress it, you can still sense it, at a sub-aware level or see it through body-language, eye-communication, smell, posture and attitude. We cannot hide who we are and what we are thinking because our thoughts translate into actions. Our actions and subtleties such as gestures reveal our thoughts. Here is something that might at first feel uncomfortable to you but that will, once it sinks in, be very liberating:

They know everything about you!

If you thought you were hiding your concern about your weight, financial situation, longing for a certain person, your boredom with them or whatever else you thought you were hiding: You are not! They KNOW. Some of them know it consciously, some of them know it subconsciously. If for example you cheated on your spouse, the slightest pang of guilt sends an energy-vibration over to him/her and is immediately received as their "intuition" or "a hunch". They will either repress it into sub-aware layers of their consciousness or they will confront you about it. If you are giving a lecture and radiating the thought-emotion "people might be bored by this"...guess what's going to happen? The vibration will influence your voice and you will radiate boredom all over the room and people will indeed start getting bored! Most of what you communicate you transfer without ever saying anything. Through who you are and what you do, you communicate. Through your eyes, body and moods you communicate. What are you communicating? Your true intentions. And EVERYBODY can see them, consciously or subconsciously. And if you pay attention, you can see their intentions too.

So let's say you had a meeting to negotiate a deal and it failed. Examine the thoughts you had surrounding the subject and the person you were meeting. If you secretly thought "What a creep he is" it's no surprise you failed.

Our non-verbal communications are a source of unconscious self-sabotage because we don't realize that people can read our thoughts. We think we can safely go "Fuck this freaking loser!" and get away with it. A thought may not be as intense as your words, but it's still being picked up by the other.

There are several ways to approach this problem. One of them is to simply become aware of the ever-babbling mind and how it labels people. Notice your neighbor. Notice how you label your neighbor. Examples:

"Really sweet person"
"I want to avoid him"
"His lengthy conversations are tiring"
"He is attracted to me"
"I am attracted to him"
Neutral (no opinion)

The first label of the list is a friendly label that will make him smile when he runs across you. How many people smile when you see them? That's an indicator of what kind of inner labels of people you have. The thought-wave "I want to avoid him" will not only be sensed by him but create that you meet him more often. So if you feel that you have that label, breathe it in and retreat your attention back to the space prior to having created that label. Did you get that? Just pull back from that label or allow yourself to view the neighbor without it. If you want, replace it with the thought "He is a funny person". See what kind of interaction that thought-wave creates. Same with "his lengthy conversations are tiring". Whether or not "He is attracted to me" is helpful or not, depends on what you want to achieve. If you actually want to get closer to him, then "he is attracted to me" is much more helpful than "I am attracted to him". Are you getting this? I just told you a secret to Flirt. Finally, if you are in a no-opinion state, you are perceiving reality and will most likely pick up their true state. When you are in neutral-mode your telepathic and empathetic abilities are the highest. Why? Because you are not preoccupied with all the "stuff" that normally goes on in the mind.

Don't take this as an invitation to try to control your thoughts every step of the way. You can't do that and that's no fun. Instead, take it as an invitation to become more aware of your conscious, half-conscious and subconscious labels and how they affect your interaction with others.

Interest

If you are interested in others, you appear to be interesting. People like you, like you. Get interested not only in the other but also in their personal fields of interest. Example: If you are looking to improve Communication flow with customers, it might also be advisable to list their particular interests when you file their name in an address book to remember to bring them up in conversation.

If you can help others feel better about life, you have excelled at Communication. Normally, once we get to know someone, the exclusivity fades and we begin taking people for granted. If you can put some effort into still treating people special, your Communication flow with the world skyrockets. Let go of all past memories of the person and treat them well, looking at them with fresh here-and-now eyes. Make others a little more important while understating your own importance.

Of course all this assumes that you have the energy to give. If you lack energy, your interactions with others will be disharmonious. So it is important to retreat to your own space regularly, to recharge, before venturing out into the world.

If you are selling something (and most humans are either selling a product, a service or themselves), your Communication must also include the demonstration of value of whatever you are selling. Make it real by demonstrating its use, listing as many reasons why your product, service, viewpoint is worth something. Transformational Communication involves saying what others do not have the Courage to say. Many problems could have been avoided by simply communicating them. I recently coached someone who has been fired from all the jobs he has ever had and we discovered the primary reason for his being fired was a lack of communication. He saw problems but did not have the courage to stand up and point them out. Thus he was not contributing to the betterment of the companies he worked for. The natural consequence was that he got fired. Courage and Communication are primary factors of prosperity. Statistical Research indicates, for example, that more than 65% of all people who ask for a pay raise get a pay raise. If you never ask, it cannot be given. Face-to-face connections are more effective than phone and internet connections. Whether you are selling something or simply want to socialize, it is always better to put yourself out there and meet people in person. In a society of people hiding behind internet-monitors that can be quite a challenge. But in a world where people have become accustomed to emails over personal contact, showing up personally can give you the "market-advantage" you are looking for. To become a better communicator, work on the expressiveness of your voice, your eyes and your facial movements. Talking to yourself or higher self in the mirror or car can warm up your speech before important meetings.

If you require practice of Courage, see if you can speak to at least one stranger a day for a 100 days in a row. That should fix the problem. If you look at the statistics of hospitals, of illness and death-rates you will notice that lonely people tend to be worse off than people who connect (this applies to those who are not lonely by choice). Connecting therefore, boosts your health and that of others.

Remember that people are easy to enchant. And you enchant them by seeing them the way soul sees them: with fascination. Don't let lack of communication denigrate the quality of your life. There are no "stupid questions" and there are no "stupid comments". Every human being is full of surprising answers to anything and everything.

Handling Difficult People

One good way of handling difficult people is to "stay with yourself", not to let them get you out of your own sense of well-being. You look at what words, actions and emotions are coming from you, not the difficult person. You retrieve attention from them and what is coming from them. The whole "difficulty" is created within you by you focusing too much on what is coming from them. But if you were to radiate a better state, their state would improve as well. Changing your reaction to a person literally changes the person. The method never fails and it is often amusing to see how well it works.

Another way of relating to troublemakers is to stay with Presence. Rather than zooming in on the content of the conversation or on their face or on the content of the problem, you broaden your attention to include the context of the conversation the general air and aura of the surroundings, so that your attention is not zoomed but open. You can observe without fixation. This will tend to clear the air – at least your own.

If a troublemaker enters your space it is in your power to do something about it, to change the atmosphere. You are not a victim of the whims of other peoples moods. Of course, going an "eye for an eye" by giving other people back what they dumped on you is a higher level than being their victim. But there is a higher level than "eye for an eye": It's called Forgiving and then Shifting Attention and sometimes that entails leaving the room.

Yet, another method of approaching difficult people is by concentrating on their eternal spiritual self rather than the narcissistic ego-self. You then not only change your own viewpoint but also radiate a different kind of appreciation that will be felt by the person. When forgiving the person you then do not excuse their behavior, words or actions but forgive them as a human being. Two people fighting is usually two hurt Egos interlocked in their mind-stories. For the fighting to stop, one of the people involved has to let go of their story, at least temporarily let go of "being right".

You – from the eyes of others

One of the quickest routes to self-improvement is to view yourself from the eyes of other people, from outside. Having someone record you on camera in normal everyday life - not in special situations, not at weddings, celebrations, lectures - but in normal everyday life may or may not be flattering to you, but it will show you reality. A reality that is neither negatively nor positively distorted. And once you know and accept reality you are in a position to allow reality to transform. I conducted the camera experiment in my early twenties. I hung up a rented security camera in my apartment and let it run every time I was home. The aim was to forget the camera and behave like I normally do. I'm very glad I did, the experience was illusion-shattering. I was not the cool jock my mind pretended to be, but pretty overweight. My body movements were not calm like I thought they were but awkward and clumsy. When other people were present there was a little more self-centeredness than I wanted there to be. But I did't know that. When alone there was a little more indulgence in pointless entertainment than there needed be. However, there were also good sides and it was not the good sides I had thought I had or had wished for but brand new realizations about myself: I was a pretty humorous and tolerant person. The kind of person you could share anything with and it would be OK. I had not seen that sense of humor and kindness in myself up til then. I rather thought I'm a really cool and good looking fellow...but far from it, I was an overweight and humorous fellow. The camera-experience changed my life for the better. I saw the points I wanted to improve.

Throughout life it can pay off to take some time to see yourself from others' eyes. It is humbling because you notice you are not all that your mind cracked you up to me, but it is also inspiring because you see you are better than that. There is a difference how you see yourself and how others see you. And the truth lies in the middle of the two.

While you are sitting there, imagine you are standing in front of you, looking at yourself sitting there. What do you feel? What do you see? What do you sense? And then imagine you are an employee, employer or customer, looking at you sitting there. What do you feel? What do you see? What do you sense?

And imagine you are a friend, spouse or partner: What do you feel? What do you see? What do you sense?

What can you accept about that person sitting there? What would you like to improve about that person sitting there?

What could you love about that person sitting there?

Judging People is Fun

Although we secretly judge people all the time, many times a day, we are always told its not good to judge or pre-judge people. That is, of course, the good thing to do - to give someone a chance to show who they are before judging them. Something important however often forgotten when we say "don't judge" is that there is also such a thing as positive judgment. Without even knowing people or giving them the chance to show who they are, I enjoy judging them positively. This type of judging has a powerful effect upon both the judge and the judged. When practicing this, you distort your perception so that you see only their best sides and the judged feel they can relax in your presence. They will feel your positive disposition and it will uplift them.

As a Seminar Coach I use this tool to influence my groups positively. I pre-judge them as "enlightened beings" who know just as much or even more than I do and who are entirely capable of becoming all they can be, who are competent, intelligent, creative. When a teacher puts trust in students, this supports them, it opens a space where they can become that! A teacher on the other hand who has too many negative pre-conceptions about students will adversely influence them. The same goes for bosses and employees, partners, parents and children and anyone else for that matter.

For this reason I have become extremely judgmental. I am full of prejudice...but in the positive sense! If I see someone struggling, my first thought will not be "What a poor idiot" but rather "He can do it". The mere thought is transferred telepathically and subconsciously felt by the receiver. This does not mean I am a fool who ignores peoples dark sides. There is nobody living on planet earth who does not have a shadow-side. If that dark-side gets out of hand in someone, I will indeed - after a fair amount of time - judge them negatively in my mind and discontinue associating with them.

As you look at someone neutrally, with no opinion or

agenda at all, you view their true nature. As you judge them positively, you notice their best sides, as you judge them negatively, you notice their dark sides. It can be fun and give you a new experience to label people positively and then see how their behavior changes accordingly, to see how much of what you experience is projected internally. By the way: If you are happy, you are more likely to see others as happy. You see the world not as it is, but as you are.

You can't change others – but you can influence them
You can't change others in any long-lasting way. Real change must come from them. As long as you want others changed you are exerting resistance in their direction - which often strengthens their resolve not to change. You can however give them the time, space and attention in which their own path can most easily unfold. Take them as-they-are and you make it easier for them to become someone better. This is how you become a positive influence on others. Through your charm you can easily influence others. Through nods and words of acknowledgement. With resistance people are almost impossible to change, but with just a little approval flowing in their direction they will much more likely listen to you or follow what you exemplify. Be it in Leadership or raising children or having a relationship or in a team...by your example, others learn the most.

It can take some real practice to overcome the tendency to say "You should", "He should", "She should", "They should". The paradox is that once you let go of needing to change others your influence on others will expand to awesome levels. You will notice they are then sometimes willing to do anything you ask. Put differently: You can either run around trying to chase butterflies with a catching-net or you can hold the scent that butterflies most like and are naturally attracted to.

Overcome Language Laziness

I recently watched a conversation between a couple that had been married for a long time but had become incredibly lazy in their communication, apparently taking each other too much for granted:

"Could you bring me that...uh...thingy...you know".
"Uh-Huh".
"And Uh...the towel-hanger thingy too..."
"Yup"

Throughout my entire stay with them, the wife was describing every second object as a "thingy" and the husband was giving extremely terse answers.
This laziness actually reflected in their choice of clothes. They had me as a visitor and hadn't even bothered to get out of their pajamas. I tried not to overwhelm them with unfamiliar concepts or vocabulary, but that clearly limited my own range of emotions. When everything is just a "thingy", not much Imagination is developed.

There are many kinds of language laziness. One of them is to continually use "fillers" such as "anyway", "actually" and "like"...as in..."Well, he was like...a really nice guy...and I was like, ok, let's try this...anyway....we got into the car and he had one of these air-freshener thingy's..."

Becoming lazy, terse or unconscious with the vocabulary and language is not only indicative of low energy or exhaustion but can perpetuate a low energy state. Putting a little descriptiveness and effort into your speaking and writing can increase your energy. Why? Because the language you use shapes what you are able to Imagine. And what you are able to Imagine, changes your energy-state, makes all the difference between Depression and Enthusiasm. The difference between public speakers, well-known actors, popular politicians, well-known authors, Casanovian seducers and normal folk is in that their language evokes images.

So let's take this lazy sentence:

"Well, he was like...a really nice guy...and I was like, ok, let's try this...anyway....we got into the car and he had one of these air-freshener thingys..."

And turn it into something more evocative:

"He was the kind of tall and handsome guy that would make me nervous if I were a fluffy little cat, but I`m more of a tigress, so I agreed to enter his private space in the form of a blue Mercedes. Because I was enjoying his ever-so-slight touch of musky perfume I did not appreciate the penetrating and artificial smell of the "air freshener" that was dangling from the rear-view mirror".

You can see how just a little more detail will evoke more image and thereby more emotion and serve to change your internal state.

When people come across as bland and shallow it's because they have stopped caring about their speech. Long-term relationships are especially prone to this once partners stop putting effort in, because they are taking it for granted, but that doesn't make for a good relationship. Any marriage can therefore be revitalized by once again putting a little more thought into the talking or by making a point of coming up with new conversational terrain to cross.

Not being fully expressive can also be a method of hiding, of not showing your true self and therefore trying to avoid being rejected. "Well, if they reject me, it at least won't be my true self they are rejecting" the subconscious seems to be saying. So by being boring, people are trying to avoid rejection...sounds crazy doesn't it? The idea behind this is if they stay unseen, nobody will attack them but this occurs at the expense of their aliveness and energy. Also remaining unseen will not give them any noticeable benefit. They will be the first ones to be laid off when a company is dropping employees. When I am in coaching with someone who is emotionally hurt, they often become weak and lazy in their expressiveness, no longer describe things in detail, no longer imagine things. This is due to a lack in energy. However, that missing energy could be regained by focusing and being more descriptive.

To get an experience of your own will, energy and lack thereof, here's an exercise:

Choose an Object in your surroundings and describe it in detail.

Did you try that? And how did it go?

Anyone who has ever tried to write fiction first encounters the difficulty of how to describe things. There are many ways to describe and express something. Quite often, the vocabulary is missing. For instance, I have a weakness when it comes to describing plants and greenery. I do not know the names of most flowers and plants. Because I speak several languages, I often miss detail-vocabulary to describe different shapes, sizes and looks and scents. To make a daily advancement in my language-power, I look up Dictionary Definitions, learn "a new word a day" and also check for synonyms to words I often use. A detailed language is much more powerful and helps to overcome mental laziness. By detailed language. I of course, mean descriptive and evocative words, not a bunch of superfluous jargon and bureaucratic gibberish.

The power of evocative language, poetry and story-telling is to increase peoples attention-spans and therefore power-of-focus and power-of-imagination way beyond that of Twitter-Tweets, so that they may give up their superficial and shallow ways of seeing and look and feel more deeply.

Change your vocabulary to bypass others' reality filters

I alter the vocabulary I use, depending upon whom I am talking to. It's such an essential piece in my communication toolkit. That doesn't mean I censor myself. I do not change the essence of what I am saying or teaching, only the wording. The medium changes, the message stays the same.

Let's say for example, I want to do an eyes-closed session with students. I'll usually say "Let's do a Meditation. Please close your eyes", but in a Business-people-setting I might instead say: "Let's do a concentration exercise. Please close your eyes". You see? The result is the same, only the vocabulary has changed. Why was it changed? It was changed to bypass resistance filters in the listener I end up doing the same thing. It's funny how the identities people wear, such as "I am spiritual" or "I am a Business Person" can sometimes predispose them to resist certain concepts and embrace others. Fortunately these days, most "Business people" are not so touchy that they resist the word "meditate".

Changing your vocabulary for others is a service, not a matter of trepidation. If you overdo this or do it with the motive of fear instead of love and respect, it turns into taboos and being afraid to "offend". So the fear-version would sound like this: "Hmmm....there is this religious person in my group. What if they don't like the word "Meditation? I am going to use the word Prayer instead. Oh, but wait...there is an atheist in this group too...what if they resist the word 'prayer'? I should call it hypnosis. Oh but wait...if I call it hypnosis they could become paranoid. Hmmm...OK, I'll skip Meditation altogether".

So while it is good to modify your words to match the culture and reality of the people you are talking to, you need never censor yourself just to comfort people's ignorance.

People are conditioned to react with resistance to

certain words. Other words have simply fallen into disrepute due to bad experiences. Being mindful of people's reality-frames is the basis of good communication. If you know how to word and phrase things, you can be quite frank, straightforward, taboo-breaking, or controversial...and nobody will mind. Neither is vocabulary-changing to be mistaken with opportunism. An opportunist changes his essence, his inner stance depending on who he is talking with. The real point is that you are not changing your principles, just the vocabulary with which you communicate them. There is a difference whether you say "You are stupid" or "Let me show you something more intelligent". With the former you probably won't reach your goal with the other person, with the latter you probably will.

By choosing the right wording you can bypass anyone's inner censor. I recall a seminar I had where there was a stereotypical "soft guy" and a stereotypical "tough guy". The soft guy had a fragile looking body, a beard, kind and sweet eyes. The tough guy had a shaved head and big muscles. They couldn't't have looked more stereotypical. Just from their looks one could predict all of their views. That's why we so much enjoy people who look one way but then think another way. They surprise us by breaking stereotypes. It was refreshing to observe how these two thought and spoke just like they looked. So when I was talking about love and forgiveness and our essential oneness the soft guy was enthusiastically nodding whereas, when I talked about willpower and how the mind dominates circumstances, the tough guy was enthusiastically nodding. I find it absolutely hilarious how you can sell anything to anyone if you use the right words. Sadly of course, the soft-guy and tough-guy will hear nothing outside of their identity-frame. Your identity limits what you perceive, see and hear. As the energy level of humanity rises, people's identities will become less rigid and they will more easily be able to digest unfamiliar concepts.

The way you talk to your parents is different than how you talk to your lover, is it not? That is not because you are being manipulative; you are being mindful of people's reality-frames. Every human being has desires and resistances. If you have an idea of what they are, you can use that to manipulate them, or you can use it to establish respect and rapport between you and the other.

As a good communicator, you are able to both respect others' filters, bypass others' filters, release your own filters and even build your own filters, depending on what aspects of something you wish to perceive. All of life is a wonderful exchange of ideas and energies, of filtering and not-filtering, opening and closing, breathing in and out, going wide and going focused.

Immune to Manipulation

Nothing is forcing you to give people the power to control your smile, your worth, and your attitude. People subtly manipulate each other every day, often subconsciously, some consciously. Knowing about various methods of manipulation greatly reduces their power over you and you become less easy to manipulate. All "being manipulated" is connected to "being reactive" instead of relaxed. What follows are six common but subtle games people play. If you are calmly present and aware, you will notice all of these games being played thus will rarely participate in them yourself.

Quick-Movement Copied by Others

Have you ever noticed that when you take your glass for another sip, a person sitting near you also picking up their glass? As previously stated, when you make a movement and someone near you copies that movement without delay, it means their attention is with you (they are subconsciously in-sync with you, which is not a bad thing) or that they currently don't have an inner position of their own. In flirt-situations we can sometimes see this play out. One person will deliberately make a sudden movement to see if the other subconsciously moves along. If the other is aware of the game, they will stop themselves from moving along as not to reveal their flirtatious intentions early on. A person who is "too much into you" will react to every single movement you make.

Over-Agreement reveals they want something from you

When someone openly or secretly wants something from you, they will tend to over-agree with you. For example, even if you tell a lame and boring joke, they might hysterically laugh. Or even if you say something uninteresting, they might nod their head in agreement. This is why Bosses can get bored with their employees - because they are surrounded by a bunch of "butt-kissers" who never disagree with them.

Over-Disagreement reveals the same

A man or woman who wants to know whether the other is "interested" in a romantic or sexual manner, simply checks if there is over-agreement or the extreme opposite...over-disagreement. With over-disagreement or ignoring or looking-away, the person is trying to disguise their over-agreement. So someone with a "good game" will neither over-agree nor under-agree but simply be authentic. On the reverse side, if you want to get someone to agree with you, agree with them first. If they disagree with you, then there is some resistance in them which can be neutralized by your own agreement. So you approvingly nod at what they say, and then bring forth your own suggestions. Your suggestions will more likely be met with agreement than if you had disagreed with them first. These silly energy-games of desire and resistance never ceases to amaze. If, of course, you are dealing with mature people, it makes no difference whether you agree or disagree and you can skip all the Kindergarten and cut to the chase.

People like Acknowledgement

Another way to bring an "enemy" to your side is to ask for their help. Why does this work? Because those who don't like you do not view you with compassion. But the moment you request their help, they are able to view you as someone in need and their heart softens. Quite manipulative, isn't it? I am not recommending you go around and use these tools to manipulate people, but you should at least be aware of them as not to fall for them yourself. Of course not all and not even half of the people who are asking you for help are trying to manipulate you. It is possible at times though and I have seen it used now and then.

In general people like being acknowledged, they like agreement and nodding and when you paraphrase and rephrase them…especially if it's not overdone. One more thing: If you are dealing with someone insecure, don't always correct them when they are wrong. We enjoy time with confident people more and it is because we can just be authentic, without needing to consider their sensitivities all the time. On the other hand, don't often censor yourself too often just to comfort others' insecurity.

Don't sign deals after Dinner

Something I've noticed people trying to pull on others is to first invite them for dinner and a glass of wine and to then close a deal or sign a contract. It is believed that in the evening, after a long day and especially after food and wine, the mind no longer has the clarity and zest it did in the morning. Sometimes manipulative people try to exploit that by offering deals when you are not in good shape. Therefore only make the big decisions when you are in a good state. Any decision made out of tiredness or emotional turbulence is bound to cause later upsets.

Price Contrasting

An old trick people pull over and over again is to contrast prices. So you might enter a shop to buy a jacket. If the salesperson is trained in price-contrasting, they will first show you an expensive jacket and then a similar jacket for a lower price. This greatly increases the likelihood that you will buy the lower-price jacket. You may not have bought it had you not seen the higher-priced one first. I know this real-estate agent who daily negotiates prices. If her actual high-price for the piece of real estate is $200 000, then she will start out at $400 000 and "generously" scale back to $300 000 and maybe even a "last offer" $250 000. That means that in the end she will get $50 000 more than the "high price". Relative to 400 000 it really looks like a bargain when it is not.

What does this mean for you? It means that you needn't always assume that you have to pay "full price" because many items are deliberately over-priced to make the person selling look "generous" when reducing the price. If contrasting doesn't work, what manipulators will do is just the opposite. They will downscale and make you "an offer you can't refuse". Once you have said "yes" to the offer, they have your agreement and think they can now make a slightly bigger offer that you will also say yes to and so forth. In sales-language this is called "getting people on yes-street". If you are a conscious person, then you don't really "need" anything and it is impossible to manipulate you. If you are aware of what is going on, you cannot be manipulated.

Someone recently sat across from me and as he was copying my body posture, he said: "I am mirroring you. That way it's easier for me to get rapport with you". I laughed out loud because once he revealed what he was doing, the game was over. In fact, the realization that he was attempting to manipulate me made me skeptical of him, instead of appreciative. So in the end, it's probably best to do without manipulation altogether and just be who you are from moment to moment. This makes you an easy person to be around.

Healing Broken Agreements

Examples of broken agreements could be:

* A broken Business contract
* A broken promise
* Relationship infidelity
* Being absent from an agreed upon meeting without apology
* Aborting a project without notifying, preparing or reimbursing those involved

An agreement establishes a bond of energy between two or more people, non-mutually breaking that bond severs the connection. If you wish to continue a harmonious and productive relationship to others, broken bonds must be healed and fixed. The telltale signs of a good private or business relationship are harmlessness and mutuality.

Courses of action depend on the severity of the betrayal. Saying "I will meet you at 6 o'clock and then arriving at 7 o'clock" is not a severe betrayal (nonetheless the person doing so is not being true to their word and will not instill confidence). Betraying a contract or relationship infidelity may be a little more severe. To heal the situation, the betrayed person must go beyond victimization through forgiveness and self-improvement while the betraying person must ask forgiveness and make amends. That's how to fix the situation psychologically and emotionally. The negative alternative to that is an endless cycle of distrust and blame

Relationship infidelity occurs when both partners agreed on monogamy. Such an agreement should take place at the onset of a relationship. It should not be hoped for, implied or taken for granted. The exception is marriage where fidelity is ceremoniously promised. I've seen relationships gone bad in which one side did not request loyalty at the onset in the mere hope the other would someday "change their minds" or out of fear that the other would disapprove. As in all other areas of life, where there was no agreement, no cheating happened.

Breaking the agreement is a break of trust and a break of a connection cultivated over time. It takes a lot of time to create that special bond but only a few minutes to break it. A common cause of infidelity is boredom or the desire for something new. That is something that could have been addressed long before the event. Hence, a more root cause of infidelity is lack of communication. All relationship problems, from the smallest to the biggest have something to do with withholding one's thoughts, frustrations and desires. Had one of you communicated "I'm bored in this relationship", it may have been a little painful, but then both would have the opportunity to do something about the situation. Since infidelity does not really satisfy the need for adventure and freedom, it will keep repeating until that need is met on a spiritual level. Trying to satisfy this need with sex with a wide variety of partners is like eating sweets in an attempt to quell the hunger. The satisfaction is only temporary and not quite as deep as that of good food.

Relationship Infidelity

One of the major blocks to healing this is the societal assumption that it is about perpetrator (cheater) and victim (the cheated on). That is a mistake. Both sides have made a number of mistakes and gone into unawareness. If you are the one who cheated and feel regret, then I recommend you follow this little energy-clean-up process to the best of your ability:

Say to yourself:

"I admit I made a mistake.(feel that)

I am sorry. (feel that)

This mistake was motivated by _____ (for example: Boredom or Anger or Desire).(feel that)

I love you. I would like to forgive myself." (feel that)

Repeat these ideas slowly and consciously until you

can actually feel and accept them.

Say to your partner:

"I admit I made a mistake. I am sorry. (feel that)

This mistake was motivated by _____. That however, is no excuse. (feel that)

I love you. (feel that)

I would like to ask for your forgiveness when the time is right for you. (feel that)

I would like to make it up to you with _____ (come up with amends in the form of action).

If you do not feel regret for your actions because your actions were motivated by revenge or if you think there is nothing wrong with having a little fun on the side that is your right. However, as in any other area in life, having agreed to certain behaviors, is not only binding as a social contract but also energetically/spiritually. The correct path would have been to approach your partner and say:
"I have changed my mind. I no longer want to live in monogamy".

In that way you have resigned from the agreement and can go about doing whatever you like. That may be more difficult than having secret affairs, but it's much more clean energetically. Every time you keep a secret, your emotional body contracts and a little bit

of your attention/energy is compartmentalized.
It's not wise to make a forgiveness request while the cheated on is still in turmoil. Wait a few days or longer. Repeat the cycle if necessary. But do not allow your partner to hold this event against you for years and years. There must be some point of closure, after they have forgiven you and you have carried out your amends. Otherwise they will hold a grudge against you for years and go on a repetition-loop where they bring it up in every argument you have. If they are unable to come to closure now, give them some time, but then, after a few weeks demand closure. Explain to them that you understand your mistake and it won't happen again but that it's not OK to keep bringing it up once amends are made.

If there is no mutual forgiveness, a cycle of blame ensues. You will then be blaming each other for all kinds of things for years to come and complaints will accumulate. The complaints are usually not related to the cheating-event but subconsciously driven by that original instance of unforgiveness.

If you are the one cheated on, I recommend this cycle of action:

Say to yourself:

"I am not a mere victim. I admit that through unawareness over time that I have allowed this to happen.(feel that)

We both are involved in letting this happen. (feel that)

I love you.(feel that)

I would like to forgive myself for allowing this to happen." (feel that)

Say to the other:

"Im sorry this happened. While I do not approve of what you did and wish that you do not do it again, I love you.(feel that)

While I do not approve of the action, I would like to forgive you as a person, as my friend, partner and lover. (feel that)

Should it happen again I will _____ (for example: Leave you). (feel that)

I accept your apology and your amends and I vow to not keep bringing it up against you in the years to come." (feel that).

Repeat these ideas until you have regained a genuine sense of peace on the matter and are ready to move on.

Once forgiveness heals the pain on both sides, you and your partner should sit down and address the root of the event. If for example the root was boredom, you should talk about how to reinvigorate your relationship, understanding that a little effort must come from both sides and that the nature of love changes over time. Like a plant that needs to be watered, a relationship needs an injection of fresh ideas and attitudes now and then. If such a mutual understanding cannot be reached, its better you both physically separate for a few months to find your own unique identities again and release preconceptions about your partner before either returning or moving on.

This is a very short section but it does contain everything needed for healing the event, if earnestly applied. In real life often it may be accompanied by longer spans of time and troubled emotions on both sides. Keep releasing those. Humans are fallible. Let go of the "perfect world" delusion and instead become more relaxed and compassionate. It's rather easy to spiral into the comfortable hubris of victimhood, blame and resentment, but don't. It benefits neither you nor your partner. In times of crisis do your utmost to maintain an air of clarity.

Broken Contracts

It would be good to list all the contracts, agreements and promises you have non-mutually broken throughout your life time. If you have had hundreds of energy-abortions this is a place to get some of your life-energy and vitality back. For each item on your list, ask forgiveness from the person you have broken an agreement with or betrayed and offer to make amends. If the person is no longer available or doing so is not feasible for some reason. then privately ask forgiveness (in meditation or prayer) and write down how you will make amends toward life (rather than the person). The word integrity relates to being an integrated being, with all your parts being whole and complete, rather than a compartmentalized, split-off, troubled being.

The next list to make is to address all instances in which you have been the "victim" of non-mutually broken agreements and contracts throughout life. For every item on your list write down what emotions you were motivated by before the other broke the agreement with you. This will, in most cases, reveal your part in it. Then, practice forgiveness for each item on the list by forgiving yourself and the other.

6
Public Speaking

In Public Speaking anyone can move from unease to calm, from dullness to zest, from confusion to clarity, and from being boring to being remembered. This is one of those subjects where it really is "all in the mind". It`s a matter of knowing yourself, knowing your stuff and knowing the audience. The more familiar you are with them, the easier it gets but what if you have never seen the audience before? Well, in this case you act-as-if you have known them for a long time.

If you have held presentations for many years then you have such a high familiarity with the subject and with people in general that there is no fear to perform. Your challenge then is not fear but boredom. If you are however insecure then simply pretend to be with a group of people you have intimately known for ages. The result is an immediate calming effect. The sense of familiarity can be increased by the way you relate to and think of others in general. If you feel alienated from people in general you won't be very fond of public speaking. You can also increase your sense of familiarity with your audience by looking right at them and breathing with them. A sense of familiarity can also be accomplished by being with people who like and accept you - and this is why fear of public speaking is usually higher before you step on stage. Familiarity can be increased by learning about what the audience you are speaking to wants. An intimate understanding of what they desire will have quite a calming effect.

When you access the truth of the soul, it has a calming effect. The soul's truth is that these people are not much different from you. By neurotic distortion - trying to be bigger or smaller than human - you tense up. If you tell yourself "I am very important, my speech is very important and the people are idiots who have to learn what I have to say" you are making yourself bigger. If you tell yourself "I am so insignificant, nobody cares about what I have to say" making yourself smaller. Both attitudes will create unneeded tension. The truth of the soul is that you are comfortable with any human. Understand this and you will never be worried about public speaking again.

If you are too concerned about your public speaking, first gain more familiarity with who you are, then with who others are, and also with the subject you are talking about. Familiarity with your subject allows you to focus on it in detail, and as you focus, all concern and worry fade away as you get into the flow of your expertise.

For those who have already overcome fear, it's a matter of finding zest, of not only having mastered a subject but also loving to talk about it. You can gain or re-gain zest by adjusting the topic of your lecture to what you more believe and enjoy. Another way to regain enthusiasm for speaking is by coming unprepared...by preparing no notes, no papers, no plan, no anything. In this way your speaking becomes a spontaneous expression of your soul. Of course, if you are in fear, you certainly need preparation to have control. On the highest level, your speech is almost "channeled" from a higher-self, without much need for rigid preparation. If this is too high for you, see if you can find a balance between memorizing or reading off script and talking without script. In the case that you do use notes or script, do not stick to them like glue. Keep making pauses between speaking, keep looking up at your audience to establish rapport.

It's easier to get your message across if it's carried by your connection with people and your enthusiasm, rather than intellectualizing. There are many artists, politicians and activists that are too smart for their own good. Their talk is so laden with abstract conceptualization that nobody bothers to listen. Much complexity may prove that you are very smart, but it will often not do much for audiences, unless that audience has a way above-average attention-span. Simplify your speech, have your message be remembered by using pictures, examples and multiple contexts. If you are inspired yourself, you can inspire the audience as well.

In some of my workshops I play a fun game called "shifting other people". You may want to try it out for yourself. The game requires two people sitting across from each other. The aim of one person is to stay serious and the aim of the other is to make them smile or laugh. It's an energy vs. energy game where the person with the strongest intent and focus wins. The person who is supposed to make the other laugh can say or do anything they want. In the group we did several rounds each and most participants were very easy to get to laugh, but some held their ground and stayed serious throughout. Those who radiated the humor felt better, those who were made to laugh felt better, but those who stayed serious also felt better because they felt the power of not being swayed by external influence. The conclusion of the game was that "you can shift some people some of the time but you can't shift all people all of the time". The game can be played for as long as you enjoy. Laughter guaranteed. You will learn that it is easier to be shifting peoples moods when they are not strongly intending to stay serious.

You can become a good orator by emulating speakers who are already great. You become like the people you admire.

When I was in my 20s I used to prepare for my seminars by listening to hours and hours of audio recordings by motivational speaker Tony Robbins. I felt that my speaking in those days was rather dull. Tony Robbins speech was energized and enthusiastic. So in order to get closer to his patterns, tonality and attitude, I simply listened to his speeches before and during my seminars. And because we become what we immerse ourselves in, my speech became more powerful.

In my 30's, my tastes changed and I instead listened to numerous other famous speakers and teachers whose tone I admired. In some of my recent seminars I have switched to listening to British Comedy instead of motivational talk. The reason is that I would like to bring more Humor into my speaking. So I will put hours of good comedy onto my smartphone, and begin listening hours before my seminar begins. I will pull out the earplugs when I reach the door of the Seminar room. Being thus tuned in to laughter and hilarity I will effortlessly communicate that mood to people and there will be more laughter in the audience.

So whatever you want to become, simply use what we could call the "Full Immersion" method. Choose someone you admire and look at them or listen to them speak for days, weeks, months. You will become a little like them. Then, once you have "borrowed their energy", you can synchronize it with your own nature and preferences. This is how you become a better orator...or anything else actually.

Charisma Training

The dictionary defines Charisma as "a compelling attractiveness or charm that can inspire devotion in others"

Sound good? Then let's examine a few components of Charisma:

1. Presence

When you are sitting or standing in a room with a group of people, you either have Presence or you don't. If you do, then peoples attention naturally gravitate in your direction. If you don't, then you are just one of the grey mass sitting in the room. You can develop this magnetic aura by becoming present yourself. Becoming present means to be "fully here and now" with the people, with the room, mindful of the peoples moods, mindful of the rooms interior, mindful of your own body, mindful of the various relationships between the people. The more mindful you are of the subtle nuances of everything happening in the room, the more you "control" the room psycho-physically, so to speak. I have coached numerous public speakers and this was always the main breakthrough point - developing presence. Presence presupposes that you are not preoccupied with other places, other people, other times, mind-stuff and so on.

Presence will improve your communication in every manner. Are you checking your phone? You're not present. Are you trying to peddle your own concerns instead of listening to what people are saying? You are only half-present. Are you telling people how great you are? You are not present. Are you interrupting others because you are eager to defend your viewpoint? You are not present. Now if interrupting others comes from-presence that's a little different, but that's not the way most people interrupt. Presence is calm and poised, an observing witness in a sea of chaotic thought that is normally present at gatherings. Is your walk deliberate? You are present. Are you commenting on someone's new hairstyle? You are present. Do you consider before you speak? You are present.

2. Tone and Voice

Voice Training and bringing flexibility into your tone is a vital part of being able to steer and direct meetings, conversations, presentations. The tone in which you say something is often also more important than the words used. "Hello", for instance, can be said in a friendly or unfriendly tone. Tone is the carrier-wave of an intention.

Proper breathing improves the tone and voice of your speech, making it more adjustable. As you become more present, you will be able to match your voice and the tone of your voice to that of the people you are speaking to (and you will also be using vocabulary that best suits them). The more comfortable and confident you feel in a group or in front of a group or with another single person, the more your voice will improve and have impact. This is a matter of relaxing your tensions deliberately.

3. Appearance

Do you actually take the time in the morning to look good? If you have come into the habit of "just wearing anything" this can take away from your charisma. On the other hand, if people notice you are mindful with your clothes they automatically assume you are mindful with other things as well. Dress for success, especially when you go to important meetings. Take the time to improve your facial and physical looks as well. Women are better at this than men it would seem. As a man you could at least trim the hairs out of your nose and ears, for example. Purify and clean yourself. You will thus have an easier time feeling better and that in turn will affect your energy-aura.

4. Be Physical

Become a physical being who practices a physical discipline. Do not live your life in your head. Do you like sports, workout, yoga, bike riding, nature, water, air? As you become more attuned to physical reality, your connection to it (and thus to others) will improve. As you are pleased with the shape of your body, your Charisma increases.

5. Be Skilled and Knowledgeable

Learn. Acquaint yourself and become familiar with a broad number of subjects and things to communicate. Don't bore people by talking about the weather. Can you recite Shakespeare? Can you speak Japanese? Can you taste the nuances of Italian Wine? Do you know which music groups are in vogue with teenagers? Are you familiar with the latest Internet inventions? The point is, do not alienate yourself from what is happening, so that you can relate to the people you meet. Also be expert at a few things. It subtly shows in your energy-field.

6. Be Joyful

Being joyless and never laughing is just a habit. You can break that habit by making a deliberate effort to laugh and smile more. You can hang up a memorizing-card somewhere that reminds you to smile or laugh more often. To talk to strangers more often. To open up more often.
Needless to say, each of these steps in and of themselves will increase your Charisma.

The Power of Voice

A voice can shatter glass or soothe someone's emotional hurt, can uplift or drag down. I have recorded thousands of audios in the last years, and have learned that my voice, as the carrier of the message is just as important as the message itself. When I had a "good voice day" I would get positive Feedback on my recordings, if I had a bad voice day…I would get no Feedback. So I started making sure my voice was "properly tuned" prior to making a recording for someone. To tune my voice, I take a few deep breaths; that's usually enough. If more tuning is needed, I sing a song. If even more is needed, I do overtone-chanting.

I've been asked many times by students who like my voice, "how I got it" and "what I do to train it". In the past I wasn't able to answer the question because I wasn't consciously training anything. I don't voice-tune before lectures and seminars. You might be wondering why: It's because in front of audiences I naturally have more energy than when sitting around at home. There, no voice-training is needed, because the inner state naturally creates a pleasant voice. We humans typically "rise to the occasion". When at home, no extraordinary voice is needed, so it's not available. Hence voice-tuning is sometimes needed before recording an audio. Also, during public lectures, the more you speak, the better the voice gets. We typically need some time to "get into the flow". Because people keep asking me, I have thought about all this a little. My most basic way of speaking, when I lecture or record meditations and in coaching, is in an Arc, as follows:

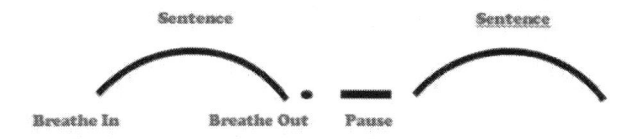

Sentence ⌢ *Breathe In* *Breathe Out* • — *Sentence* ⌢

In normal cases I make sure I have enough breath before speaking. Breath makes your voice more full and resonant. Lack of proper breathing can make it high-pitched and too tight. My voice often gets lower at the end of a sentence or after a number of sentences. I make a pause then the next arc begins. Going lower at the end sounds more confident and pleasant. Making pauses tends to give what is said more weight and allows some mind-space for reflection. People who speak in one straight line without arcs and without pauses tend to make their audiences sleepy. It is a common mistake of public speakers to speak too quickly.

Of course, I don't always speak with this arc. Without some variation and conscious change, anything can get boring. The picture above merely shows the stable basis from which I make changes. When I ask questions, the arc is reversed, the voice rising at the end. I will sometimes not make pauses, make longer pauses, speed up, slow down, change voice, or change tone. This makes for more entertaining speech (whereas too much variation causes confusion). These changes in pace and tone indicate that a speaker is "in conscious control" of his or her own state. A piece of advice to all public speakers: Don't seek to control the audience's state; seek to control your own. That will set the tone and atmosphere of whatever event you are speaking at.

Your emotional state changes your voice and inversely your voice also changes your emotional state. When I was younger, I worked as an English teacher for some time having applied this principle also. After new vocabulary was introduced in the context of some story, I read the words out loud and had students read after me. In time, I started reading the words in different accents, moods and voices. I noticed that this improved students ability to learn because it brought a shift of energy into the room. Ever since those days I apply "voice change" if I want to change either my own mood or that of an audience. If you are feeling down, you usually have a voice to match that. If you want to change "feeling down", try speaking like someone who is energetic and vocal and you will soon notice your emotions following your new voice.

There are some voices that annoy us because they are spoken on a frequency very different from our own. I am not only talking about sound-frequency here but also consciousness-state. These states are not "better and worse". Many insist that they are and continually ask me how to reach a "higher level". However, I feel each level has a specific purpose. A golf player has different golf clubs for different purposes and he chooses the appropriate one. That doesn't make a particular golf club "better or worse". In any case, each consciousness-level is associated with certain typical beliefs, preferences, goals, smells, places, vocations….and even certain typical voices and intonations. If someone's voice is radically different from where you are right now, you may not like it. When I watch a movie, for example, I will not find any of the voices objectionable, but if I am meditating and hear someone else watching the movie in another room, I might experience the same voices as horrible.

I live in Europe but travel abroad regularly and every time I do, I notice quite a difference between the average European voice and the average American voice. My European-Ear experiences a particular variation of the American voice, known as "uptalking" or "village girl voice", as slightly annoying". "Uptalking" is when the end of a sentence is intoned like a question rather than a completion. In the last few decades this kind of speaking has become more common in the U.S. It was originally mostly American women who spoke this way, but you hear more and more men doing it too. So if someone is saying "I am a good swimmer" they`ll make it sound like a question: "I am a good swimmer?" It makes the speaker sound insecure or as if he is trying to hold the listeners attention rather than completing a statement. It takes a few days of being in America until I get used to it again so it no longer bothers me.
 Some foreigners consider the "Uptalking voice", as an indication that someone is stupid. And while that's certainly sometimes the case, I have found that most "uptalkers" just do it by habit – because that's what they grew up with, that's how people in their area talk. It often stops sounding stupid when you get used to the frequency. When I return back to Europe after

weeks or months, the voices sound harsh, cold and hard in comparison (exceptions: Italy and France, which usually sound melodious, no matter who is speaking). So it takes a few days until I get used to the frequency. Globally speaking, conscious people enjoy changing their tone. So they will neither always uptalk, nor downtalk, and not even soft talk nor hard talk. They will have a voice appropriate to the situation. Some frequencies I may never get used to: In the summer I sleep with my windows open and every Monday at 6 a.m. in the morning, garbage collectors come by and, for some odd reason, shout their lungs out, waking me out of my sweet blissful sleep. It's difficult to sync the vibratory states of "restful sleep" with people shouting. I have often wondered: What are they shouting about? It's not like collecting the trash requires a whole lot of communication. Another speaking technique I have used subconsciously, is voice-emphasis. These are some examples of how emphasis can completely change the impact of what is being said:

"I am satisfied with the latest feedback by our client". Now let's check how the meaning of this sentence is changed depending on intonation:

"**I am** very satisfied with the latest feedback by our client".
"I am very **satisfied** with the latest feedback by our client".
"I am very satisfied with the latest feedback by our **client**".
"I am very satisfied with the **latest** feedback by our client".

"I am **very** satisfied with the latest feedback by our client".

You can see how the entire mood and context changes through slight changes in voice. Often, such subtle alterations can be a source of amusement as people pick up on subtle nuances being communicated without being said.

When making very important points, I usually slow down the pace. In my last seminar I said:

"Your self-image, the way you see yourself, determines your success in life".

Note here that I didn't say that the way it is written here. I slowed down and built in several small pauses, as follows:

"Your SELF-IMAGE….the way you SEE….yourself…determines your success in life".

What underlies all of this change of voice, pace, emphasis is being conscious. You let your voice trail unconsciously for some time, and then, to initiate change, you implement consciousness. Incidentally, this is the way life works best too. You let life flow and go effortlessly on automatic for some time, but when things start getting out of hand, you regain conscious control of your reality.

7
Presence

Attractiveness and influence are not only determined by looks and status but by the state of Consciousness. Heads turn when you enter the room or walk the streets not because of fame and beauty but because of your energy-field. Even if you are not blessed with good looks, a slim body or fame, you can develop the kind of aura where people say "I just don't know what it is…there is something about her". Such magnetism is a spiritual quality that can help you gain command of business situations, score a flirt, hold lectures and entertain dinner gatherings.

To experience Presence, be in touch with what is going on here now. Your mind is not wandering around in some story about the past or future but with what is going on in your current surroundings. When you are sitting in a meeting and you catch your mind wandering off, that's alright, but if you want to be appear more present to others, you have to bring your attention back to the room you are in. Instead of wanting to be elsewhere, your attention is fully dedicated to the people around you. Attention is extroverted and highly interested. The body is not tense, the mind is not worried, you are completely at ease. That's a good starting point for that special aura called "presence". People then realize you are completely and totally here…with all your parts. You fill the room with presence.

In various social situations tension prevents people from being present. They are more concerned with what others think about them or how they look than with the present moment. Letting go of such considerations and relaxing your muscles on the outbreath will help you ease tension and become more present. Exaggerating the importance of a situation can also lead to unnatural tension. If you happen to strike up a conversation with Scarlett Johannson or George Clooney on the plane, the mind tends to project more meaning into that, than if had met some "normal" stranger. The ego would then appear and presence is lost. So while taking your meetings with other people as being important, it is not necessary to inject too much seriousness. When talking to celebrities, in order to reduce the tension I simply downgrade their importance in my mind by imagining their normal-human sides, not the Hollywood-projected side. Instantly, I am able to relate to them and talk to them as if talking to an old friend.

Notice how easily your attention goes internal, toward mind-stories and away from the external. That is natural, not something you have to control or overcome. However, for purposes of Presence, you can learn to extrovert attention when needed. When you talk to someone and go internal or become preoccupied, it's as if you have cut the connection and others can sense that. Rather than internally calculating possible advantages or disadvantages of the encounter, just be present with the other person. For the purpose of Presence, let go of any Expectations and that includes projected

Expectations. A "projected Expectation" is an expectation you think someone else has of you. The truth is that you don't really know what – if any – Expectations others have of you. It's only the mind creating all kinds of suspicions and scenarios. Let go of it all and become Present. Let go of everything you think you know and just be-with-what-is.

Move less, slower and more deliberately. Cease all fidgeting, foot shaking, scratching yourself, making nervous gestures. Stop shifting back and forth in your seat. Stop constantly walking back and forth or pretending to be busy doing something. Stop playing with objects on the table. Not in general, but for the times you wish to increase your presence. Being unmoving or less moving indicates that you have conscious control over yourself – which implies conscious control over your reality. As a teenager I tried this in disco/club settings several times. I would either dance or stand there unmoving but open. Friends of mine would walk back and forth, react to every impulse. Stability is magnetic, that's why sooner or later people started gathering around me, trying to strike up conversations. There is a big difference between not moving because you are shy and not moving out a state of Presence. The latter radiates power. There is also a difference between "moving because you are nervous" or "moving deliberately" and between "being silent because you are afraid" or "being silent out of calm". One repels, the other attracts.

If you're on a date, the way you use your hands is indicative of the way you will treat him or her. Pay some attention to the way you touch and handle objects such as the table, the coat, the glass, the knife and fork, the door, etc.

In being present you simply accept what-is, as-it-is. There is no concern with what might happen, what might not happen, what must happen, what must not happen. There is no attempt to try to get rid of something, heal something, solve something, or change something. All of those things take you away from Presence. Neither are you looking for "the right thing to do or say" because what "the right thing to do or say" reveals itself naturally from moment to moment. That could be something entirely different than what was the right thing to do or say yesterday. Finally, your presence grows even more when you radiate states such as:

Interest
Respect
Appreciation
Gratitude
Amazement
Reverence
Love

Silent Radiance makes people laugh

What follows is a very-high-energy exercise that will leave you feeling fundamentally transformed for the better. Go to a park or a cafe, planning to sit there and watch people for hours. It should be a place where you can see hundreds of people an hour, some passing by, some standing, some sitting. Intend to sit there for several hours, with infinite patience. If you are sitting in a cafe you may want to switch cafes or switch over to a bench after an hour or two as not to arouse the suspicion of waiters.

Begin this Meditation by externalizing attention and having keen interest in the people walking by. Put and keep your attention on them exclusively, with very little attention on yourself or your concerns. During the next hours you are not important, you are not interesting, you are not the center of the world. Other people are. Look at their faces, their clothes, their mannerisms, listen closely to their voices and words, study their behaviors. Be more interested in the world out there than ever before in your life but remain relaxed about it. There is no effort, expectation or hard concentration involved. You will notice that any sort of expectation you develop (for example, wanting a certain person to return your gaze), interrupts your flow. So view people without pressure, without desire, without resistance - completely free. You will notice some resistance to certain people. If that is so, you can either shift your attention to someone else or release it and focus more closely on that person. Reduce preferential looking to some extent. There will always be natural preferences for one person compared to another, but you are trying to reduce labelling somewhat as not to get side-tracked from the Meditation.

Do not worry about people thinking you are strange for holding your gaze on them this long. You will learn that most people are not even aware of it. Especially in busy cities or towns (where you should be doing this exercise), they will just pass without noticing you. Some people who are aware of other things than themselves (which is rare!) will notice that you are looking at them but they will keep moving. And then there are some people that will return with a smile or give back the appreciation. You might find that these are often older people who are no longer stuck in the prison of the Ego but indeed interested in what is going on around them.

At the onset of your Meditation you may or may not feel appreciation toward the people passing by. Do not force this. Appreciation will arise of its own after some time. You simply maintain keen interest in all people walking by. You do not get fixed on one person but maintain free attention. Once in a while you examine the people sitting or standing near you. Some people you examine for a few minutes, most you examine for a few seconds. As your patience and relaxation increase, your love will increase and you will notice a shift in your state that gets stronger by the hour. You are now seeing people as your soul sees them.

As you continue keen interest in the world and its people you will not only learn everything there is to learn about humans, you will also start radiating on a higher frequency. People will start noticing you differently. You will begin feeling a sense of laughter. Don't be surprised if you start laughing for no apparent reason and people around you start looking at you in a strange way; you will see the comedic hilarity of the human condition.

The last time I did this I was sitting in a street-side sushi restaurant on North Michigan Avenue in

Chicago. After about two hours of sitting, people who walked past the Sushi Bar and noticed my state, began smiling and laughing themselves. I saw that some entered the restaurant just to sit close by. The waiter had gotten impatient at my sitting, came over to me and said, "Will you have anything else, Sir?" I looked at him and he immediately drew a smile that was suppressing laughter. I looked over to another table and immediately drew smiles from there. People recognize higher states of Consciousness and when you are "in state"; your mere gaze can make people laugh.

You will notice that after completing the exercise your state may return back to normal…but it will not return quite as low as it was before. You can go out "sitting and gazing" any time again and get into the field anytime again. The smile that arises from this exercise is not a forced or fake smile. It does not even require your face to go along with it. It is an inner radiance and glow that makes anyone who sees it laugh.

Augmented Presence

Isn't it ironic that computer-based products such as "Google Glasses" that will diminish our perception and presence are being called "Augmented Reality"? They should rather be called "Decreased Reality". Real "Augmented Reality" is when you wake up to and participate in what is happening right now. A distracted and preoccupied mind does not make for presence. Full presence is very much related to well-being and energy. For instance, if you are truly dedicated to a task, the here-now, past and future cease to exist – and with that, all worry ends. Being fully present allows you to feel reality as it unfolds, empathize with yourself and others, and truly make use of the day.

Diminished reality is actually more widespread than commonly known. Yesterday I went shopping for groceries and decided to do it in a fully present state of being. I extroverted attention and let go of all desire or memory of elsewhere. I became fully aware of others, taking note of them with calm interest. When touching goods I felt their texture and handled them with care. This of course led to reality becoming truly augmented and lighting up. Colors became more beautiful and the whole supermarket-experience thus more enjoyable.

Suddenly though, that supermarket started playing that remade song "American Pie" by Madonna and that quickly and easily triggered a loss of Presence. Well, presence was not entirely lost because I could see what the mind was doing right then. The song moved me away from present moment and threw me back into the year 2000, to a time when the song was released and played everywhere. Memories of what I was doing in 2000 arose and my mind started wandering around there. At that time I was conducting fairly boring Seminars for the Siemens Company. I did not much enjoy those Seminars, so the song triggered some of those emotions (and I didn't like the song either).

Such "loss of presence" happens often. I'd say that

we are not fully present most of the time. Sometimes we are taken away from the here-now by external triggers, such as that song. To break the conditioned-response I could decide to stop thinking about those days every time the song played. Or I could decide to associate it with something else.

Memories only replay in the mind if the present moment is believed to be less interesting or intense than the past moment. So if the memories/emotions had been too intense, I would have to look for something more interesting in present-time, something or someone irresistibly beautiful. If your loss of presence were very intense, you could splash cold water over your face which would inject instant present-time awareness and have the troubled emotion subsiding (want to release painful emotions rapidly? Return to present-time!) Or I could hold a gun barrel at your head, which would wake you up to present-time right away. I`m kidding of course, I would not hold a gun to your head, but I am not kidding about danger-situations calling you to rapid presence. Any situation of great danger or great beauty induces presence. Sometimes our higher-selves send us accidents in order to call us to more presence. It would not have to send us accidents if we were more present to begin with.

What you try to hide is amplified

If you are on a date with a potential partner and you try hiding your chubby thighs, you can be sure they will be noticed. If you are giving a presentation to potential investors and are terrified about revealing certain statistics, you can be sure someone will ask about them. If you are on vacation and afraid someone you know will see you in your bathing suit, they probably will. If you are at a job interview and try masking your ignorance about something, your ignorance will be detected and made bigger than if you had simply admitted it. If you are worried to death of being rejected, you will be…very often. If you strongly resist being judged, you will be judged harshly. If you are among friends and impose a Taboo on mentioning a certain subject, they will keep bringing it up and make fun of it. Conversely, if they don't bring it up, they will keep thinking about it nonetheless. If you very much fear appearing awkward in front of others, you will. If you want to avoid being boring at all costs, you will appear as someone boring. Whatever you try to hide is amplified.

Many of the coaching requests I receive from people regard overcoming stiffness in social situations. Many would like to feel less stilted, artificial, tense, embarrassed, and self-conscious. The key to transcending awkwardness is to allow yourself to be awkward. The key to transcending your fear of mistakes is to allow yourself to make mistakes. The key to transcending being boring is to allow yourself to be terribly dull. Resistance is what amplifies and attracts that which you resist.

Before you have that important meeting or important date, you can first realize that, compared to Infinity, nothing is important. From an Infinite Perspective you can neither possess anything nor get rid of anything because all is part of one Infinite Field. So as you can neither have nor lose anything, there is no need to worry about anything. You see, having or losing, possessing or getting rid of something, imply a limited Universe. If the Universe is unlimited, you can't put anything outside of the Universe, hence you can't get rid of it. Nor can you add anything to the Universe, you can't possess it. Everything is already there, always has been, always will be. This simple metaphysical understanding has the power to liberate you from any problem at all.

If you feel awkward in social situations, it is likely because you are strongly judging other people. Because you are subconsciously judging them, you think they are judging you. However, most people are too busy or too self-conscious themselves to be judging you. Almost nobody is actually judging you. You are judging them, and that is when you start to feel shy in their presence. So if you want to feel more free and light in the presence of others, feel more of your own Being, stop judging people, and cease assuming what they are thinking of you. Most of them are not thinking of you at all (If you want people to think of you, think of them first).

As what you resist will persist, let go of seeking approval from others. People do have the right to disapprove of you. If you think people aren't allowed to disapprove of you or criticize you, you are like a little dictator who opposes freedom of thought and freedom of speech. Whatever you try to hide is amplified. So if you try to suppress people's right to criticize you, they will criticize you to your face and behind your back. If you think others should not think badly of you, you are really concerned with censoring their freedom of thought. That's an interesting way to see it, isn't it? Many people are secretly totalitarian dictators without realizing it. Give up resisting others' disapprovals. Accept that nobody owes you approval, that nobody owes you love, or that nobody owes you an explanation of their thoughts. When you stop resisting people's disapproval, two interesting things happen: You will experience much, much less disapproval and you will also see that it's almost never personal. People's judgment of you have more to do with who they are than who you are.

If you are still afraid of being boring, then be boring deliberately. Tell the person whom you are having conversation with: "I am a rather boring conversation partner". They will probably laugh! If you are afraid of stuttering, stutter deliberately and on purpose several times. If you are afraid of your secret affair being discovered and find yourself unable to release the fear, then disclose and expose your secret. Does that sound difficult? It is. It's a temporary pain for a long term gain. When there is nothing you need to hide or protect from, nothing to suppress or resist, nothing to avoid or run away from. Your light shines very brightly because no more energy is wasted on suppression.

10 Ways to Become Fully Present

Where there is presence, there is no worry about past, future or elsewhere. There is only crystal clarity. With that said, these are simple ways to become more here-now, more present:

1. Just sit and do nothing for a few minutes

The easiest thing in the world…to just sit and do nothing for a few minutes, is actually very difficult to modern people. They are always driven, always thinking, always planning the next step, always doing. So just sitting there and doing nothing feels quite empowering, because one is no longer at the effect of expectation or pressure. Release any guilt, time pressure, and impatience. Sit there, breathe, and BE. You should be fully present at least within a few minutes.

2. Describe objects in your surroundings

While you are sitting, standing or walking, describe objects in your surroundings. How would you describe the various things you see? How would you describe them to someone who isn't present, so that they can imagine them? How would you describe them to a blind person? One thing that most people will notice is that they sometimes lack the vocabulary to give fully satisfying descriptions. In doing this, you also become very focused, very present and the world starts looking brighter and more interesting.

3. Walk Around and Touch Objects in your Surroundings

If you are overwhelmed, stressed out, have a headache, feel exhausted or any other form of non-presence, you can take a nap. Or you can go around and deliberately touch various objects, feel their texture, size, temperature, weight and shape. A few minutes of this will make you much more here-now and much less worried or fearful. Presence has a stabilizing effect on your emotional state.

4. Intend and then Do

For a few minutes, announce everything you are going to do, before you do it. If you are going to get up, say, "I am going to get up". Then do it. This alignment of thoughts and actions increases your Presence.

5. Look at Beauty

Deliberately looking at something highly aesthetic or something new you that haven't seen before helps you become present. It is preferable when these are actual objects, buildings, plants, animals and humans, but they could also be pictures of such as well. You will be fully present within only minutes. Do not look at too many nice things all at once, but linger with your attention for a little longer (60 seconds +) at one thing.

6. Shower, Bathe, Swim or Splash Water over your Face

Some cultures, such as the Tibetans, do not wash themselves with water (they use other means of cleaning themselves). The reason is, that water washes off many of the energies you picked up throughout the day or night. For us non-meditating westerners, this is good news. By taking a shower we do not only wash our physical body and skin, but also some of our non-physical energy residue. That's why showering, bathing or swimming also feels mentally refreshing. People in a state of panic need only splash cold water over their faces to once again become present. Confused housewives need only take a shower to regain some of their poise. Stressed out business people need only go for a swim to return to calm.

7. Focus on a Task

Choose a task…any task…and intend to focus on it fully and completely, regardless of how you feel initially. Within a few minutes time you start becoming present and feeling better.

8. Feel the Emotion behind the thinking

Too much thinking indicates too little presence. To slow down your thinking (worrying!), feel the emotional state behind the thinking. Gently shift attention from the thinking toward the actual feeling in the body. Breathe with it and relax. Release. You'll feel more present within a short time.

9. Do something courageous or something that you have been putting off out of timidity

Taking that courageous step you have been putting off makes you fully present instantly.

10. Observe without Expectation

Sit and observe your thoughts or the world passing by while you reduce expectation, desire, and resistance. You'll feel more clear and present within minutes. This sense of presence can be expanded by increasing the time you sit and observe. I sometimes do this for hours. "Taking a walk" is also a method of "observing the world" and always recommended for more presence.

Conclusion

I trust you have enjoyed this book and marked sections that are relevant to you for re-reading in the future. Learn the concepts presented in this book but don't obsess over them or overthink them. Too much thinking inhibits free communication. Now go out and communicate. Make friends, strike deals, fall in love or use your energy to make the world more pleasant and interesting.

Frederick Dodson, 2014

For more information visit the authors' website at www.realitycreation.org

Printed in Poland
by Amazon Fulfillment
Poland Sp. z o.o., Wrocław